Thank you Joe!

BROKEN BORDERS, BROKEN PROMISES

Todd Stippler

TODD STAPLES

BROKEN BORDERS, BROKEN PROMISES

How Porous Borders Are Robbing America's Future

TATE PUBLISHING
AND ENTERPRISES, LLC

Published by Tate Publishing & Enterprises, LLC
127 E. Trade Center Terrace | Mustang, Oklahoma 73064 USA
1.888.361.9473 | www.tatepublishing.com

Tate Publishing is committed to excellence in the publishing industry. The company reflects the philosophy established by the founders, based on Psalm 68:11,
"The Lord gave the word and great was the company of those who published it."

Book design copyright © 2013 by Tate Publishing, LLC. All rights reserved.
Cover design by Samson Lim
Interior design by Mary Jean Archival

Published in the United States of America

ISBN: 978-1-62563-086-5
1. Political Science / Commentary & Opinion
2. Political Science / Law Enforcement
13.01.31

DEDICATION

To the valiant sentinels who are on the ground, in the air, and on the water, making the United States of America a safer place. Please know you are not alone. The prayers of many patriots are with you petitioning for God's guidance and protection over you and your families. May you take comfort in his word:

> It is God who arms me with strength and keeps my way secure.
>
> 2 Samuel 22:33 (NIV)

AUTHOR'S NOTE

100% of the net proceeds of this book are being donated to causes to secure our border, support our border law enforcement, and foster ideas to reform our failed immigration system.

SPECIAL RECOGNITION

The Statute of Liberty used in the cover design was taken from a graphite on Bristol paper drawing by Janet Staples, www.janetstaples.com.

ACKNOWLEDGMENTS

Great team members make for winning teams. Any book worth reading has been helped along and inspired by more people than can ever be listed.

To the members and staff of the Texas Farm Bureau, Texas and Southwestern Cattle Raisers Association, Texas Wildlife Association, South Texas Property Rights Association, and my Realtor family at the Texas Association of Realtors, thank you for always and forever standing up for the rights of landowners. Thanks to the individual land owners whose testimony, in spite of fallacious criticisms, provide constant and true testimony of the daily atrocities occurring right here in the USA. Your efforts to call attention to the need to protect the rights of those who own a piece of our great state and nation cannot be overstated. Without your inspiration, this book would have never been written.

Texas Department of Public Safety; Texas Border Sheriffs and their deputies; local law enforcement and city police departments; and our Border Patrol officers, National Guard, and other federal partners are our nation's front line of defense. Thank you for courageously defending our country and for protecting everyday citizens from the lurking dangers of a drug war. Your leadership and courage signal strength and resolve—a strong message to convey to any who chooses to harm our citizens. Your efforts are fundamental to winning.

Besides my family, the most constant person in my political life has been my chief of staff, Shannon Rusing. Shannon, along with my longtime senior policy advisor, Kelley Faulk, dedicated a tremendous amount of personal time and talent to ensure this book could become a reality. Drew DeBerry, my deputy commissioner, joined our team six years ago and has proven a trusted ally with an unusual talent to blend good policy which results in good politics, and always works to ensure we consider every angle with an eye on accountability. Bryan Black and Veronica Obregon launched www.protectyourtexasborder.com and their work has been essential in telling this story. Jason Modglin, Neal Carlton, James Bernsen and a team of others have worked to call attention to this ever-growing problem and have worked on solutions. The entire team at the Texas Department of Agriculture has been an inspiration because of their love of Texas. J.K. Patterson traveled extensively with me as I listened to the stories of countless landowners. Cody McGregor has been steadfast in pushing this issue regardless of the political costs.

My wife Jan has been a continuous sounding board, an idea developer, sentence completer, walking thesaurus and a tireless proofreader. Her partnership in life is beyond description. Simply put, she makes every aspect of life fun. Our children Brian, Jonathan, Jared and Elizabeth, and their families, are whom we fight for each day. And I must say that there is no better encourager than my mother, Carol, who always gives far more than she ever expects in return.

CONTENTS

FOREWORD

What a difference a year makes. In November 2011, Commissioner Todd Staples asked General Barry McCaffrey and I to do a study of Texas border security in an effort to put a military-strategic lens on the problem. For the next few months, our report was the subject of a varied and creative counter attack made by the Texas media, the Department of Homeland Security, and the Congress. Both Barry and I endured a very uncomfortable three-hour grilling by members of the Texas Congressional delegation that attacked our intentions as well as our integrity. Our expose has been followed by nearly a year of silence by the media and politicians.

This political silence, I believe, is due to a realization among politicians in Texas that we were right all along. General McCaffrey and I also hypothesized that Texas' problem was fast becoming America's problem and, again, we were right. The unattended intrusion of the cartels into all of our cities and many of our towns has become an unstoppable cancer on the welfare of those most vulnerable. When we wrote our study, we proved that the cartels had infected over 400 municipalities in America. Today, the number is 2,000 and climbing. Murder rates driven principally by cartel-driven gang-on-gang violence is spiking in cities like Chicago and Los Angeles, both a long way from the Texas border.

Yet even after the election, the message remains obscured by a hidden blanket of media silence. The Federal government continues to "cook the books" on the true extent of cartel intrusion into our daily lives. Sadly, subjective evidence is growing that the cancer of cartel money is corrupting our local law enforcement and city governments to an unacceptable degree. The cartels have taken their campaign of criminal intrusion well into the United States and like all previous mafia-style efforts have succeeded in gaining entrance into legitimate businesses. They have bought properties abandoned by farmers and ranchers who have been driven off their properties by coercion from criminal gangs. A spike in investigations and indictments among federal agencies again speaks to the fact that inattention has led to a growth of corruption that, sadly, may well be unstoppable.

Even more threatening is the international expansion of the cartels. Retired Colonel Robert Killebrew in his most recent study for the Center for New American Security concludes that cartel evil has gone global, infecting regional states such as Guatemala, Honduras, and Venezuela (as well as Mexico). Likewise, the cartels are expanding into Europe and farther into the Middle East and Asia. What started in the soft underbelly of the United States now threatens the world community.

Another frightening and looming threat is the growing connection between cartel intrusion and global terrorism. It is not coincidental that the largest Iranian embassy in world is in Venezuela. Dozens of mysterious Middle Eastern men are captured and returned across the border to Mexico every year. We have no idea how many of these potential terrorist sleepers gain entry undetected. Recent press reports of cartel violence in the United States paid for by terror states is not coincidental. The Department of Defense spends billions on missile defense to protect us from nuclear Armageddon. Yet the odds of a nuclear strike carried across our borders in trucks are a far more likely proposition.

Most distressing is the chronically dysfunctional approach of this administration to the growing threat of cartel intrusion. So far at least we have seen no serious effort to improve our defenses to meet the clear offensive by cartels and their American gang allies. Too often the cartel offensive is linked to illegal immigration. The border protection agencies point to a drop in immigration and to a reduction in crime. To be sure, the cartels profit from illegal immigration but don't depend on the flow of immigrants to feed their hunger for profit and influence.

Resources are not the problem. Recognition and commitment are. Now that the election is over, the Administration no longer has a motive for low balling the problem and humiliating those who know the facts. Now that our foreign wars are winding down, it's time for us to pay attention to wars closer to home. Just a small fraction of the money spent in Iraq and Afghanistan could go a long way to stopping cartel and gang intrusion inside our cities. The Armed Services have learned at great pain how to build coalitions, tutor military and political leaders, and train and advise alien armies in the Middle East and South Asia. Now it's time to redirect these talents to missions closer to home.

We have bought at great expense technologies capable of detecting border intrusions between Pakistan and Afghanistan. Now it's time to adapt these technologies to detect intrusions across our own borders. We have built a generation of warriors who know how to fight at the small unit level. Sadly, too often drug criminals are better trained and equipped to move, communicate, and fight than our own front line law enforcement.

Let's defend our borders. Let's do a better job of protecting citizens now besieged by the evils of the cartel-gang coalitions. Let's take what we have learned in foreign wars and apply those resources and skills to winning at home.

I strongly suggest to our political classes, particularly those representing the border states, to give up trying to shoot the messengers. The evidence of failure is growing so compelling that there now are too many messengers to shoot. I hope the citizens of these states join with those who have the evidence and demand action in Austin and Washington. Let's lobby those in charge to take this fight to the enemy with aggressiveness and commitment.

In some ways we are already too late to the battle against the cartels. There is far more pessimism here than optimism. The cartels and their criminal gang allies are winning and profiting and corrupting. But we must try. The war that was in Asia is now within the heart of America. Please help us to act.

—Maj. Gen. (Ret.) Robert H. Scales, PhD

PREFACE

ONE LANDOWNER AT A TIME: HOW IT ALL BEGAN

Two issues have dominated the pleas for help I have received from farmers and ranchers near the Texas-Mexico border: border security and immigration reform. Both are issues of universal consequence, but one reached a heightened level of priority in late 2010 and early 2011.

Border security is a matter of private property owners' rights in Texas. Our state is unique in that the vast majority of land is in private hands rather than owned by a governmental entity. Throughout my career, I have been a strong proponent for the protection of private property owners' rights. This pursuit will never end, but I believe it reached a climax to date when I teamed up with the Texas Association of Realtors, Texas Farm Bureau, Texas and Southwestern Cattle Raisers Association, Texas Wildlife Association, and many other private property owner advocates to accomplish broad reform of our state's eminent domain laws both in our state's constitution and statute.

After initial reform legislation fell victim to a gubernatorial veto in 2007, I formed an even closer working partnership with our state's leading land stewards. Together, we coordinated a comprehensive legislative and voter awareness campaign that helped Texas legislators pass a proposed Constitutional amendment that was later presented to all Texans as Proposition 11. In the November 2009 elections, Proposition 11 was affirmed by Texas voters by the most overwhelming margin of any on the ballot that year.

Leading up to the next legislative session in 2011, the coalition continued its momentum and held strategy sessions and public opinion campaigns calling for sweeping reforms. We met with the governor and his staff repeatedly to hammer out differences, real or perceived. Senate Bill 18 ultimately passed and was signed into law. I believe it has been the reputation I've developed on private property issues that led to many Texans seeking my assistance on border security matters.

Shortly following the passage of Proposition 11, homeowners and landowners along the Texas-Mexico border began contacting me, seeking relief from a threat to their private property ownership rights far more complex than eminent domain.

As an elected official, each and every policy matter brought forward by a constituent has its own compelling magnitude. But few have the immediacy of life or death.

When I first began to hear of how Mexican-based drug cartels were menacing families and businesses here in Texas, I admit it was hard to comprehend the enormity of the problem I have now come to understand. While not as flaming as Moses' burning bush, God sent me a few signals to help.

Signal 1. Rushing to the airport to catch a flight, my staff e-mailed me that a South Texas landowner had called my office stating that he needed to speak with me immediately. I knew only of this person by name and reputation. He is a pretty big operator and plenty self-sufficient. He had never really needed my assistance or anyone else's on any matters. I was puzzled at the sense of urgency being conveyed.

After getting through security and finding my gate, I started returning calls. The rancher began with "Staples, you have got to get something done." He proceeded to tell me of the aggressive actions of the drug cartels and how landowners are fearful for their families to return to and work on their very own properties, which some have held in continuous ownership for generations. I asked him if he would come in and meet with some of our state law enforcement and federal officials. He said no. The risk of retaliation for standing up to the cartels was too great. I had no doubt he would do whatever was necessary to defend himself if confronted directly, but he could not bear for his family to become an intentional target because of his overt actions.

Signal 2. Just shortly after 7:00 a.m. on January 26, 2011, I took a phone call that changed everything. The previous day, I spoke to the Texas Farm Bureau Annual Leadership Conference in Austin. My speech covered a number of topics, including a strong emphasis on the privilege of owning land in Texas and the rights afforded to private landowners by Texas law. Shortly after my speech, my deputy commissioner, Drew DeBerry, received a text message; one of the farm bureau's state leaders needed to relay a story about one of the greatest crises facing private property owners today.

The events that unfolded next have had a strong impact on my public service career ever since.

Evidently, my speech about private property owners' rights connected with some recent events this South Texas property owner had experienced. Dale Murden, Texas Farm Bureau District 13 state director, described to me in alarming detail how his and his neighbors' private property rights had been violated by an intruder far worse than eminent domain: Mexican drug cartels.

The cartels had plans to utilize the property for their smuggling operations due to the location and the cover the sugarcane provided to hide them from the law enforcement's view.

ENOUGH IS ENOUGH

The moments that followed that January morning phone conversation with Dale Murden are a little foggy to me today. But I clearly remember an overwhelming sense that something had to be done. These incidents banded together the isolated and seemingly disjointed stories I had been picking up over the previous year.

Harboring a high level of anxiety following the call, I left the room and spent several minutes alone in my office. I considered the basic principles upon which my public service has always been based and defined. With the clarity reflection brought me, I then returned to my staff. We had to do something. We could not stand by while our nation's sovereignty was, and is, being attacked right here on Texas soil.

The strategy was to identify the appropriate role for the Texas Department of Agriculture and to roll up our sleeves and get to work. I did not want the department attempting to perform law enforcement or security operations. Our state's local law enforcement does a fine job with the resources they have, and they receive their operational support from the Texas Department of Public Safety at the state level. The Texas Department of Agriculture has a statutory mission to promote Texas agriculture, which I take seriously. This means helping defeat barriers to the success of any farmer, rancher, or other business that helps deliver our food supply, whether that be a boll weevil, lack of workforce, or a gun-wielding drug cartel member.

I also immediately contacted the director of the Texas Department of Public Safety, Steve McCraw, to request a briefing on border security threat assessments and operations. My staff was briefed later that same day by the Texas Rangers at the Border Security Operations Center (BSOC).

As January 26 came to a close, we had developed a plan for the Texas Department of Agriculture to shine a light on this problem that is being ignored by some and hidden from by others. To do this, we would fight rhetoric with the actual realities like the one Dale Murden shared that morning. This would be done via the Internet, the press, and any other medium we could use to tell this story. Within a matter of weeks, www. ProtectYourTexasBorder.com was up and running and was receiving an outpouring of support and testimonials from Texans who are tired of the smoke-and-mirrors rhetoric of "safety" they hear from Washington. The

Washington words fly in direct contrast to the realities of intimidation and invasion they face daily.

We conducted many landowner listening sessions aided by Roland Garcia, Special Ranger of the Texas and Southwestern Cattle Raisers Association, and relied on the resourcefulness of Texas Rangers and Border Patrol working on the front lines. We listened intently to members of the Texas Border Sheriff's Coalition. A police chief in one of the cities (whose elected officials mostly do not want to address the violence publicly) said in a private meeting that the situation is not just bleeding; it is hemorrhaging. And by the nature of the testimonials, the story turns out to be more real, gruesome, and appalling than any law enforcement reality television show.

My goal is to provide adequate protection to the men and women who grow the food and fiber upon which our state, country, and the world depend. These land stewards demand and deserve relief from the terror inflicted by the drug cartel members, and this reprieve can only come in the context of broader reform that ensures the border is secure and legal movement along our southern border is prioritized.

There are many interests, many critics, and many philosophies, but I urge you to read on with an open mind and heart; consider the realities of the border and immigration problems that face our nation and their implications on our economy and particularly the consequences of inaction on the next generation as they seek to inherit the promise of America.

BELIEVE BULLETS OR WASHINGTON SPEAK?

Bullets fly as a ranch foreman's truck is riddled with penetrating rounds of lead; he is injured by the exploding glass shattered by the brutal assault. He barely escapes with his life, only after doing what any fierce Texan would do—defend himself. The assailants flee like cowards when the foreman, though outnumbered, returns fire. He meets deadly force with deadly force—all in broad daylight and on what once was a quiet, leisurely Sunday afternoon.[1]

A farmer flees his land after witnessing armed men stalking through his private property. His pace is quickened because in his gut, he knows there is no other explanation than they are drug cartel members. His fears are confirmed as he returns the next day to find the locks on *his* gates on *his* land cut and replaced with new locks—an iron-clad sign of who is in charge.[2]

Sugar mill workers are burning their fields to harvest their cane, a common annual occurrence in the lower Rio Grande Valley. Four unknown individuals drive up on four-wheelers dressed in black military-type uniforms. The thugs warn the workers to be gone in two hours. No questions, no blinking; just a stare down with an unspoken message: you don't want to suffer the consequences![3]

Two ragged trespassers approach a rancher asking for water and food. Texas ranchers know the heat and stress of the rugged border country can be a killer and compassionately extend aid. While taking this brief break, they inform the rancher they have a friend who is hurt and needs help. The rancher goes back into his house to gather supplies, notify the local sheriff, and put a pistol under his jacket. Extending a hand of compassion doesn't mean the other hand need be empty of an equalizing force. When the rancher and the two men arrive at the isolated location where the friend was supposedly left, the travelers scatter, running in panic, when they hear the sheriff's vehicle approaching. The sheriff and rancher survey the area; there is no friend. Among the brush, they find tracks where a gang of men had been staked out. The sheriff recognizes the setup—the rancher barely escaped being kidnapped.[4]

These stories are real. They didn't happen in Iraq. They didn't happen in Afghanistan. These particular events did not happen in Mexico.

These atrocities occurred in the Lone Star State, and unfortunately, they are not isolated incidents. They are part of an alarming trend where the rights of our fellow Texans and the sovereignty of the United States of America are being threatened.

You almost have to see it for yourself to believe, and you can. They are documented, along with other firsthand testimony, on the website ProtectYourTexasBorder.com.

Transnational criminal organizations headquartered in Mexico are at the center of these attacks. To establish their supremacy in a black-market world, they launch daily and nightly incursions into the Land of the Free and the Home of the Brave.

And what is Washington's response? Broken promises.

Secretary of Homeland Security Janet Napolitano declares the border is safer than ever.[5] Barack Obama—the president of the United States of America, the leader of the free world—comes to Texas and makes lame jokes: "Maybe they'll need a moat. Maybe they'll want alligators in the moat."[6] The workers and landowners who have been victimized are mocked and even blamed.

This is no laughing matter. People's lives, property, and livelihoods are at stake.

We don't need deception, derision, and disparagement. What we need is the government of the United States of America to fulfill its promises.

Article 4, Section 4 of the United States Constitution says it is the federal government's job to defend us from invasion. Whether you choose to categorize the events as invasion or domestic violence, our land, our state—our country—is under assault.

> The United States shall guarantee to every State in this Union a Republican Form of Government, and shall protect each of them against Invasion; and on Application of the Legislature, or of the Executive (when the Legislature cannot be convened) against domestic Violence.

When these promises are broken, people die. We need our nation's leaders to fulfill their clear constitutional duties, not push contraceptives onto faith-based organizations against their religious conscience. We need action, not jokes. Mr. President, if you don't believe our farmers and ranchers, ask the family of Brian Terry, the border patrol agent killed in the line of duty with guns supplied by our own federal government. Ask the lady I sat with during the State of the State address in the Texas Capitol chambers. Her name is Tiffany, the widow of David Hartley. She witnessed her husband's shooting while the two were jet skiing on the open waters of Falcon Lake, which stretches across the border between the United States and Mexico. Ask the law enforcement officers fired on by drug cartel members while patrolling the Rio Grande.

At a press conference held shortly after an assault on our law enforcement officers, skeptics challenged the Texas Department of Public Safety about the number of times our officers were fired on. In clarifying how our officers were attacked and the volume of force used by those who placed their lives on the line defending our sovereignty, members of the press corps questioned as to why DPS would fire at someone three hundred times when you were fired on only a few times?

My response would be "We only fired back three hundred rounds because that's all the bullets we had!"

I am not an advocate for vigilantes. I am an advocate for vigilance—alertly watchful to avoid danger.[7] The danger is here for all who will see; the border is broken. And the federal government's failure to act is resulting in broken promises that will span generational, social, and racial divides.

These incidents are a sad commentary on the disconnect between Washington, DC, and the real world. So what else is new?

I BELIEVE IN THE PROMISE OF AMERICA

In his book *1001 Events That Made America: A Patriot's Handbook*, author and historian Alan Axelrod chronicles the many events that shaped, cultivated, and nurtured the embryonic United States of America. There were bold decisions, painful defeats, moments in our nation's history we wish we could forget, and beautiful patriot dreams that were turned into reality and set our grand land on a pathway to prosperity.

Patriot Benjamin Franklin's actions and vision are a testament to the opportunities available to every soul who catches a glimpse of the enticing concoction of freedom and liberty mixed with enterprise and ingenuity.

1775

In 1775, Benjamin Franklin was elected to the Second Continental Congress.[8] Most of us are aware of his role in building our nation, but what many of us forget are his many other contributions to business, the humanities, science, and society.

No longer in school, twelve-year-old Franklin took to the streets selling products printed in the shop of his older brother James. His brilliance shone through early as he covertly delivered letters to his brother's print shop supposedly penned by a fictional widow named Mrs. Silence Dogood. He confessed at age sixteen that he was the actual author, which did not impress

James. The tensions between Benjamin and his older brother never subsided, and Franklin took a bold step as he became a runaway to Philadelphia at the age of seventeen to avoid occasional beatings by his brother.[9]

For young Ben, in the eighteenth century, there was no federal social safety net in the colonies, and there were few opportunities for a formal education. Mere daily living could be a struggle for the estimated 475,000 inhabitants[10] who were carving out a life and society. Hard work, independent studies, and smart thinking were rewarded. Industrious pioneers worked to take advantage of a growing population and bourgeoning world trade through shipping across the open seas, all while wrestling with a continuously oppressive kingdom who sought to maintain unilateral control of their distant countrymen.

Franklin embodied the promise of America and is an example to others *of all that is possible in America if one is alert, works hard, and remains open to opportunity. His is a classic American story.*[11]

1975

A ninth grader in rural Texas enrolls in the Future Farmers of America (now called FFA), a national youth organization focused on teaching leadership development and the technical and life skills of agriculture production. The FFA, at the time of this writing, has grown to 557,000-plus members nationwide.[12] This young, seemingly average, relatively quiet yet idealistic Greenhand (most basic award from the FFA) student is from a middle-income family and shares with his teacher some of his goals he would like to accomplish only to be told that he doesn't have the resources, talent, or ties to excel in FFA. In essence, keep your station in life.

Little did the teacher know the true assets held by the student and his family: high standards, strong faith, and a belief in the promise of America. With limited resources by worldly standards, the student achieved the highest level of accomplishment in the national organization, the American Farmer Degree. In the face of the teacher's discouragement, in 1981, I watched my friend, Michael Bennett, walk across the stage at the National FFA Convention in Kansas City, Missouri, to be one of ninety-one[13] Texans that year to be conferred the prestigious American Farmer Degree. To date, there has been only one other student from our high school to reach this pinnacle.

Beginning with no family trust or inherited seed money, today he owns several hundred acres of land and operates a successful cattle operation in East Texas. With no family connections, today he is a manager of a successful financial brokerage firm, is a leader in his community, has helped countless individuals through benevolent acts, and is an influential member of his church. From being told goals were too high to reaching high standards, Michael demonstrated the promise of America is alive. Faith, character, and work ethic were the only ingredients.

This too is a classic American story.

2013 & BEYOND

These classical American stories are rewritten every century, every decade, and every day in our great nation. Each generation faces its own challenges, and border security and immigration are only a few facing us today. The promise of America is the constant that binds us. It is an opportunity afforded to each generation that has come before us, it is the opportunity we enjoy today, and it is the opportunity we must preserve for our children and their children. The United States is a sacred trust that must be protected, propagated, and passed on if it is to remain possible. It cannot be bottled and sold, and it cannot be harbored and hoarded; it must be fanned and allowed to flourish.

No better representation of the promise of America can be found than the Statue of Liberty. From her conceptualization as a commemoration of American-French partnership in the Revolutionary War, to her unwavering stand and ultimate survival of the United States through the Civil War, to what is embodied in her actual image (a seven-point crown, flowing robe, and raised torch), Lady Liberty exemplifies the possibilities of a free America.

The sonnet "The New Colossus" was added to the statue site in the early 1900s, extending the promise of America to new waves of immigrants:

> Give me your tired, your poor, Your huddled masses yearning to breathe free, The wretched refuse of your teeming shore. Send these, the homeless, tempest-tossed to me, I lift my lamp beside the golden door![14]

I believe in the promise of America. I believe this promise is worth protecting; the American Revolution is not over, and it continues to evolve today. Patriots in the twenty-first century struggle for freedoms from a government that is too bloated, a government that is too powerful, too debt ridden, and too eager to usurp the rights of families by fulfilling the assertion that problems must be solved by government rather than through individual initiative. Lady Liberty offered hope based on effort, not help based on the taking from one to give to another.

The challenge for Americans today, and for those who follow in the future, is defining the promise of America in an environment that seems to increasingly favor government solutions over personal initiative. How will we balance the concept of self-governance our founding fathers ratified in 1788 through the adoption of our Constitution with the lack of self-sufficiency that is woefully demonstrated in our nation today where 70.5 percent of federal spending is being directed toward dependence-creating programs of some sort?[15]

Will Americans in our generation revolt from the screams of a vocal few who call for a government big enough to solve all of our problems, even those that we don't have? Will we resolve to reform our government to become effective enough to protect our rights and small enough to be held accountable to respecting the philosophy that built the most powerful economic engine the world has ever known?

YOU MATTER

The responses to these questions will be written by you, and the answers will impact how our nation replies to challenges represented by an increasingly dangerous border and the many immigrants who simply seek the golden door.

Is our nation mature enough to solve our illegal immigration problem and insecure border in a manner and style that upholds the rule of law while showing respect for human dignity? Will you be the one to pave the pathway to prosperity by upholding high standards and by combining the need to solve the problems of our day with the necessity of ensuring America continues to be the *land of the free, the home of the brave*, and the land of opportunity? What will the promise of America be under our watch? The evolution of the American Revolution continues today.

A RISING TIDE LIFTS ALL SHIPS

Americans are truly blessed. For all the flaws critics may choose to highlight, there is no other country that provides the opportunity for individual advancement and a respect for human dignity and rights like the USA.

But we don't live in a bubble, and the state of our neighbors impacts us. There are many reasons we should care about the well-being of Mexico, but chief among them is our trade relationship with our southern neighbor. Billions of dollars pass legally through our ports to Mexico. Our ports are our gateway to the world, to legal trade, to legal immigration, and to transportation. Americans must grow to embrace the trade that provides our jobs, our sales tax dollars, and our underlying economy.

Few countries rival Mexico's importance as a trading partner for the United States, and Texas. According to trade data from the US Census Bureau, Mexico is the United States's number 2 export destination for all goods. In terms of total US trade, aggregating imports and exports, Mexico ranks our third, behind only Canada and China. Two-way trade in 2011 totaled more than $450 billion.[16]

The top ten countries in total trade were ranked as follows:

| Canada | $597.4 billion |
| China | $503.2 billion |

Mexico	$460.6 billion
Japan	$195.0 billion
Germany	$147.5 billion
United Kingdom	$107.1 billion
South Korea	$100.1 billion
Brazil	$74.3 billion
France	$67.8 billion
Taiwan	$67.2 billion

For all goods, Mexico is the United States's number 2 export destination and number 3 source of imports. Canada is the nation's number 1 export destination and number 2 source of imports. China is the nation's number 3 export destination and number 1 source of imports.[17]

According to a report by Arizona State University's North American Center for Transborder Studies (NACTS), in 2010, trade with Mexico sustained almost six million jobs in the United States.[18]

The report entitled "Realizing the Full Value of Crossborder Trade with Mexico" provides a comparative perspective about the importance of US trade with Mexico. The report provides this fact: US sales to Mexico are larger than all US exports to Brazil, Russia, India, and China *combined*, as well as all *combined* sales to Great Britain, France, Belgium, and the Netherlands.[19]

A chart prepared by NACTS details how twenty-one US states rank Mexico as the number 1 or number 2 export market. Mexico continues as Texas's top trade partner.[20]

Top U.S. States Trading with Mexico (millions of U.S. dollars)

U.S. State	Mexico as Export Market #	Exports Value	Imports Value	Total Trade
Texas	1	$72,370	$78,982	$151,351
California	1	$21,002	$32,753	$53,755
Michigan	2	$7,428	$28,150	$35,578
Illinois	2	$4,267	$8,383	$12,651
Arizona	1	$5,055	$5,630	$10,685
Ohio	2	$3,500	$5,549	$9,049
Tennessee	2	$3,040	$3,666	$6,706
Mississippi	2	$1,195	$4,343	$5,538
Pennsylvania	2	$2,387	$2,823	$5,209
Wisconsin	2	$2,010	$2,910	$4,920
Missouri	2	$1,302	$2,540	$3,843
Iowa	2	$1,833	$985	$2,818
Kansas	2	$1,281	$761	$2,041
Nebraska	2	$1,314	$369	$1,682
New Hampshire	1	$1,050	$570	$1,620
Colorado	2	$590	$644	$1,233
Arkansas	2	$544	$584	$1,128
Oklahoma	2	$432	$653	$1,085
New Mexico	1	$429	$635	$1,064
South Dakota	2	$340	$45	$385
North Dakota	2	$166	$48	$214

Source: NAFTA Trade Office with Data from U.S. Department of Commerce

An excerpt from the NACTS report provides a good overall synopsis of the need to place a priority on our strategically important trading partner and to modernize the physical connections that facilitate the trade.

> Much Opportunity, but the Real Work Has Only Just Begun
>
> The poor infrastructure, the inadequate staffing levels and the heavy focus on security that prevails at the U.S. – Mexico border have cost both economies billions of dollars in gross output annually. It is past time for our shared border to begin to meet today's demands, acting as a facilitator and conductor of lawful flows of goods, services and people across our nations

so that we may capitalize on the full potential of our partnership. If a billion dollars' worth of trade crosses the U.S.-Mexico border on a daily basis now while sustaining six million jobs, imagine what could be accomplished with a truly 21st century border.[21]

With an improved Mexican economy and a reduction of the narco traffic and trade and violence, I can only imagine the mutual benefits for both of our countries in terms of a better quality of life and enhanced opportunities.

A pilot project that offers a glimpse of the even greater possibilities is the joint initiative of Brownsville, Texas, USA, and Matamoros, Tamaulipas, Mexico, known as the Bi-National Economic Development Zone (Bi-NED Zone). This concept was introduced to me by Dr. Juan Hernandez, a native of Ft. Worth, Texas, and considered the catalyst that linked Governor George W. Bush and Governor Vicente Fox, which ushered in a new era of US-Mexico relations as each became the president of their respective countries.

Bi-NED is centered on capturing the economic benefits of strong trade by establishing a collaborative planning and communication structure capitalizing on, among other concepts, industry clusters, integrated transportation nodes, and enforcement policies.

The Border Trade Alliance, a nonprofit organization comprised of both private and public sector national leaders, is focused on the job opportunities and benefits from enhanced international trade. They seek to strengthen the ports to enhance legal trade and include both Mexico and Canada in their efforts.

As *legal* trade grows and flourishes, a tremendous by-product for the American people is that *illegal* activities (of all kinds) can continue to be squeezed out. While Texas politicians only rarely quote Californians, a statement by David Shirk, director of the Trans-Border Institute, University of San Diego, bears repeating: "Widening the gates would strengthen the walls."[22]

BROKEN PATHWAYS

L et's be honest—border security and immigration are hijacked by some in the media and extremists from across the political spectrum. They use emotion and incendiary rhetoric to shift the focus from the real issues (protecting landowners and creating job opportunities) to a story of class warfare, racism, or party bashing.

Plain and simple, there are chapters in our nation's history and paths we have traveled we would like to forget. But in forgetting, we ignore the lessons learned, and we dishonor the lives of the individuals who suffered, bled, and died. Let us grow from these experiences so that our history gets richer with each chapter. *The Life of Reason* by George Santayana offers this wisdom: "Those who cannot remember the past are condemned to repeat it."

HAVE YOU MET JIM CROW?

One hundred years after our country fought a divisive war that separated our nation, residual animosity centered along a racial divide still percolated throughout communities in America. Our legal system strained under the burden of ensuring the words "all men are created equal" were more than paper and ink because they had been protected and paid for with flesh and blood.

The Supreme Court of the United States of America ruled constitutional "separate but equal" doctrine such as in the 1896 case of *Plessy v. Ferguson*, which led to decades of legalized discrimination known as Jim Crow laws. Landmark statutes passed by the United States Congress, such as the Civil Rights Act of 1964 and the Voting Rights Act of 1965, finally put Jim Crow to rest, but it couldn't and didn't mend the deep wounds inflicted.

However, laws do not change attitudes. Only a resolve to rise above it can lead to true respect for all mankind. Sadly, Martin Luther King Jr. was martyred for the cause. But his famous words of "I have a dream. I have a dream that my four children will one day live in a nation where they will not be judged by the color of their skin but by the content of their character" have deep meaning for Americans today, almost one-half century later.

This vision of King's describes a philosophy that is shared by most Americans: a dream of being judged by the "content of our character," not our zip code or the size of our bank account. It reflects a system of beliefs that continues to guide our nation, an attitude that is still hoped for and strived for, and words that are repeated today—words repeated because they symbolize that dreams can become realities in the United States of America.

WWII: THE BEST AND WORST OF AMERICA

Volumes have been written, scores of movies were produced, and untold celebrations and parades have honored the heroism displayed in World War II. But many of us don't have to look beyond our own families to know that we have been touched by someone from the Greatest Generation. Whether fighting on the front lines, working in the absence of a father or brothers to feed the family, or enduring rationing to make resources available to support the troops, Americans who lived during those almost four years played a unique role in our nation and the world's history.

CHOKED UP ON FRENCH FOOD

I coughed, pretending to choke on something in the meal to cover my emotions at breakfast one morning in France as my wife Jan and I sat at the table, guests of the Paris International Agricultural Show. A dairy farmer from Normandy was explaining his milking operation, and I interjected that my father-in-law, Frank Wendel, had spent some time in Normandy in the 1940s.

Silence surrounded the table for what seemed like an uncomfortably long time. He said, "I want you to know...there has been no American flag burned in Normandy. My father taught us of the sacrifices made."

My eyes well with tears and my heart swells with pride each time I reflect on this encounter. Jan's dad was one of four brothers serving simultaneously during the war, and he received the Purple Heart and other commendations for his service. He and his brothers all returned home safely, with no parades or fanfare, to resume their lives and build their families. We never realized that his legacy would cross borders and generations and have such a strong influence on a man he never met, but for whom he risked his life.

REMINDERS OF HEROISM ARE FOUND IN UNLIKELY PLACES

Speaking at a President's Day dinner for the Falls County Republican Club, I had the privilege to meet and visit with W. D. "Bill" Walker Jr., who is said to be the last surviving Aggie (former student of Texas A & M University[23]) to parachute on the Island of Corregidor—a big deal in our nation's history and certainly for all Aggies. The battle on Corregidor continues as inspiration for all Americans and is recognized at Aggie Muster, a solemn and annual tradition where current and former students gather each year to remember fallen classmates, which led to these words in the poem *Roll Call for the Absent:*

> Softly call the Muster,
> Let comrade answer, "Here!"
> Their spirits hover 'round us
> As if to bring us cheer!

April 21 of each year is not only the anniversary of the Battle of San Jacinto where Texas won its independence from Mexico, but it is also a date when Aggies muster, a precedent established by General George Moore together with twenty-five men during the Japanese siege of the Philippine island. These men knew it could be their last, but they were committed to fighting until the end. Bill Walker was class of 1944, but his graduation was delayed because he left college early to fight for his country, as did many of his classmates.

Bill was part of the Second Airborne Battalion, 503rd Infantry Regiment.[24]

It is because of uncompromising and selfless sacrifices that freedom prevailed. Our debt to the Greatest Generation can never be repaid.

FROM HONORABLE SERVICEMEN TO DISHONORABLE ACTIONS

Our patriots must always be remembered for their unflinching dedication, but our generation can also learn from times of our history that were not so honorable.

Many who comment on the World War II era gloss over the internment of Japanese-Americans. Neither Peter Jennings and Todd Brewster's book *The Century*, nor *The American Nation*, second Edition, by John A. Garraty give substantial ink to the "cruel and unconstitutional incarceration of Japanese-Americans." Garrarty says the placing of 110,000 Americans of Japanese ancestry in confinement was done so "simply because of a totally unjustified fear that they might be disloyal."[25] Jennings and Brewster detail how rumors of cooperation with the enemy (cutting directional arrows in fields to guide the bombers overhead) by people of Japanese descent to aid the enemy led to an attitude of distrust that carried beyond WWII. They say "Americans simply did not want to be tricked again."[26]

While Jennings/Brewster call the relocation and internment unconstitutional, Garraty points out the actions were upheld.

The Supreme Court, generally in this century so vigilant in the protection of civil liberties, upheld this action in the case of *Korematsu v. US* (1944).

He goes on to write, however, "In Ex parte Endo...the Court forbade the internment of Japanese-American citizens, that is, of the Nisei, the second-generation Japanese who had been born in the United States."[27]

Young men fighting for their country, innocent people victimized because of their ancestry. So much to be proud of, so much to learn from.

LAWS HAVE TWO FACES

Syndicated columnist and author Walter E. Williams, John M. Olin Distinguished Professor of Economics at George Mason University, unmistakably details how race was a factor in laws, ordinances, and policies implemented during the Industrial Revolution and how they were primarily designed to limit competition to the benefit of existing workers and unions. Dr. Williams's book *Race and Economics: How much can be blamed on discrimination?* should be a good reminder to look beyond the circumstances of our day and recognize the consequences of our actions. He wisely states, "Compassionate policy requires dispassionate analysis. Policy intentions and policy effects often bear no relationship to one another."[28]

Dr. Williams theorizes that minimum wage laws actually reduce opportunities for low-skilled laborers by artificially pricing workers out of the market.[29] He proposes government pricing of labor led to displacement of workers as the wage policies led to mechanization and the elimination of human labor positions.

In discussing occupational and business licensing, he cites Adam Smith's *The Wealth of Nations*:

> People of the same trade seldom meet together, even for merriment and diversion, but the conversation ends in a conspiracy against the public, or in some other contrivance to raise prices.[30]

Dr. Williams's examples of policy decisions and their adverse outcomes are demonstrated through a case study of New York City's decision to regulate and license taxicabs. The net effect was the enrichment of those who got in early, higher prices for the traveling public, poorer quality service, and discrimination of those who desired to enter the profession because of artificial barriers to competition.

From licensure of cosmetologists to using licenses to exclude minorities from trades and other employment opportunities, to unionization as a form of protectionism, to adverse impacts of laws in the home-lending industry, Dr. Williams's book certainly proves Adam Smith's point as well as his own that "policy intentions and policy effects often bear no relationship to one another." [31]

APPLYING THE LESSONS TO IMMIGRATION

We all know we have an immigration problem, a dilemma that can only be resolved if we shrug off the emotional debates that polarize and incapacitate us and tackle the real issues. Those who wish to limit the number of workers who are eligible to enter the United States legally and suppress competition in an effort to keep wages at a higher level are actually supporting development of a competitive, lower-priced black market. Competition is natural; if it isn't recognized in a legitimate structure, it will manifest in a shadow economy.

Either we will have companies in America that create jobs in America and that pay American taxes and support the American economy, or we will eventually drive those employers to other countries with a sufficiently competitive labor force, lower taxes, and fewer regulations. Or we will drive those businesses underground where they subvert our rule of law, engage in unethical business practices, and put people in danger of mistreatment.

For all the good that NAFTA (North American Free Trade Agreement) has brought to the USA, Canada, and Mexico, it hasn't been without pain along the way. In my own hometown of Palestine, Texas, there are shuttered buildings. Once home to garment factories that provided domestic jobs, the real estate now sits empty or has been converted to other nonmanufacturing uses because the economics of sewing and producing clothes changed dramatically after the passage of this landmark trade agreement.

Jobs will flow to where they are welcomed. The "welcome" indicators are those that allow for a profit in a competitive environment where people and businesses have options.

This cannot be repeated often enough: all Americans who want to work should have that option first.

My own father worked in a glass manufacturing plant for thirty-six years. I worked there myself for a short time while working my way through community college and serving as a Texas State FFA vice president. It was hot in the factory. It could be dangerous working in the factory. The shift work never let your body adjust to the hours of the day.

It was a great job! It provided a good life for our family. It was an economic engine for our community.

The factory closed in 1984, and our community has never fully recovered from that closure, coupled with other dramatic shifts that occurred in our state and national economy in the late 1970s and early 1980s.

The point is, our immigration laws must find a balance that is needed for our workforce so that we can protect and preserve the employment opportunities here domestically.

Just like the exodus of jobs from America to China and India that has occurred over the last few decades, policy decisions we make today will have consequences for the future. Let us have that "dispassionate" analysis that Dr. Williams described as we seek to secure our workforce and our borders.

APPLYING THE LESSONS TO POLITICS...
AND OUR LEADERS

Throwing political elbows and verbal wrestling matches are said to drive some away from participating in the political process. However, jockeying for position and power is not a new phenomenon that sprang up in the era of modern television; TV just delivers it in 24-7 news cycles in living color.

Modern conversation seldom includes the tales of Aaron Burr's pistol skills and his duel with Alexander Hamilton during the early hours of the day in Weehawken, New Jersey, which resulted in Hamilton's death.[32]

The halls of Congress are traveled by noble men and women such as Vermont Democratic Republican Representative Matthew Lyon and Federalist Representative Roger Griswold of Connecticut. Griswold verbally insulted Lyon, and Lyon spat in his face. This led to the two dueling with a cane and fire tong. Lyon was said to have been re-elected to Congress while serving a prison term.[33]

The most widely known political rivals are likely our nation's second and third presidents. John Adams, representing the Federalists, and Thomas Jefferson, a Democratic Republican, struggled for control of the new nation in the 1800 presidential election. Adams was limited to one term for many reasons, including divisions within the Federalists themselves, and particularly, Jefferson's ability to capitalize on the discord.

"Don't waste a good crisis" is attributed to former congressman and White House chief of staff and now Chicago mayor Rahm Emanuel. In politics, people have often been accused of saying things they never even thought, but YouTube has done wonders to instill accountability. A transcript of the quote shows Emanuel actually said, "You never want a serious crisis to go to waste. And what I mean by that is an opportunity to do things you think you could not do before."[34]

In the late 1700s, the Federalists Party certainly didn't waste the XYZ Affair. President John Adams sent an envoy to negotiate peace with France. As history records it, French foreign minister Charles Maurice de Talleyrand-Perigord kept the American delegation waiting for weeks. During the passing days, he sent three agents—X, Y, and Z—to extort a little pay-to-play money from the American ambassadors. Outraged, the emissaries departed immediately. When the news of the scandal made its way to the American public, many Federalists called for a Declaration of War. A compromise with France was not reached until 1800.[35]

A crisis it was for the burgeoning republic, and *"the XYZ affair gave the Federalists an opportunity to attempt to silence the political opposition."[36]*

History confirms the passage of a series of laws in the summer of 1798 as the Alien and Sedition Acts.

According to *An American History*, third edition, the acts having the most visible and forceful actions that literally are credited with being a part in motivating voters to action and playing a role in the outcome of elections are the following:

1. *Naturalization Act.* This "increased the length of time a foreigner was required to live in America before qualifying for citizenship; it was designed to hurt the Democratic Republicans since most new immigrants joined their ranks after becoming citizens."
2. *Two Alien Acts.* These "empowered the president to expel aliens if he believed it necessary for American security."
3. *Sedition Act.* This "made it illegal to instigate a conspiracy against the government and to publish any false, scandalous and malicious criticism of the government or its top officials."

Government should and does amend old laws and pass new ones to address legitimate crises and remove obstacles. However, too many times, legislative actions actually result in installing more barriers and hurdles than they remove. Government must resist the uncontrollable urge to regulate ourselves away from free market solutions.

Establish boundaries? Yes.

Insist on transparency, accountability, and fairness? Absolutely.

But we mustn't allow ourselves to be conditioned into believing government can automatically come up with better, more efficient, and effective solutions than the private sector.

Under the "lessons learned" category from history's classroom, we cannot lose sight that this era of controversial political posturing, coupled with the threat of new wars, led to the demise of the Federalist Party and the blossoming of the Democratic Republicans. In fact, voting in the presidential election was so partisan the question was not whether Jefferson had defeated Adams for the presidency, but whether presidential candidate Jefferson had outpolled his own vice presidential candidate Aaron Burr. It took thirty-six ballots in the House to determine that Jefferson would serve as our nation's third president. Of note, in the general elections the Democratic Republicans picked up forty seats in the House of Representatives, giving them a solid majority.[37]

IS TODAY ANY DIFFERENT?

Seeking the rapidly growing Latino vote is more than a pastime for the two major political parties. Proposed workforce and immigration solutions are immediately judged by the media and political spinsters on how they will influence votes. The Democratic Party continues a philosophy of "never wasting a good crisis" and has seized on developments that will influence the outcome of the general elections.

The Supreme Court of the United States (SCOTUS) June 2012 decision on Arizona's immigration law was pounced on from all sides. The most publicly debated portion of the law was sustained by a unanimous vote, that being the portion that "requires state law enforcement officials to determine the immigration status of anyone they stop or arrest if there is reason to suspect that the individual might be an illegal immigrant."[38]

To further undermine state's efforts to act in the absence of clear federal enforcement of immigration laws, President Obama's Department of Homeland Security sent a "directive to federal agents in Arizona reminding them that to be consistent with the administration's priorities, they should not pursue deportation of illegal immigrants who have not committed serious crimes or are not repeat offenders."[39]

Even during the closing days of the court's session and in anticipation of the Arizona ruling, President Obama held a press conference announcing a significant change in US immigration policy. The first paragraph of the June 15 *Washington Post* story by Peter Wallsten captures the moment:

> President Obama said Friday his administration would stop deporting some illegal immigrants who were brought to the country as children and have gone on to be productive and otherwise law-abiding residents, forcing the emotional immigration policy debate into the forefront of the presidential campaign.[40]

The evening news was inflamed with tearful testimony from young Latinos sharing heart-wrenching stories. The moving tributes were followed by reports of Latino voter registration drives. Coincidence?

Republicans were quick to point out the president circumvented Congress and the Constitution by sidestepping laws in efforts to seek political gains.

Ironically, I had released just the day before a workforce reform, immigration overhaul, and border security policy initiative that was adopted by fifteen state agricultural commissioners and secretaries (SASDA), which is hoped to be a framework for broad and strategic action by our federal government. While some of the elements of what the president proposed are contained in the SASDA proposal, the executive order does nothing to secure our border or deal with the difficult issues to bring a permanent solution to a problem that was made dangerously worse with his politically motivated decision.

Why is it politically motivated, you ask? For the first two years of Obama's administration, the Democrats controlled the White House and both chambers of Congress. Immigration reform was a ripe issue. They failed to act then. However, as Latinos expressed frustration with the president's policies, it became clear the unemployment rate for Latinos was 3 percentage points higher than the national average;[41] he invoked the most emotional elements of any immigration reform in order to shift the debate in the direction his political operatives suggested. The election results of November 2012 confirmed the desired result was achieved as President Obama received historically high levels of the Latino vote.

DEFINING THE CRISIS

As a former small business owner, real estate appraiser, broker, property tax consultant, and rancher, I tend to analyze issues and problems from the perspective of economics and personal responsibility. As an elected official, this means I weigh policy decisions based on how they will impact the pocketbooks of our families and our individual liberties.

For me, immigration and border security are important because they impact national sovereignty, trade, workforce, job creation, economic competition, and private property owner rights.

DEFINING THE CRISIS IN TERMS OF WORKFORCE

"If fifty commissioners, secretaries, and directors of agriculture cannot agree on the immigration and workforce reforms so desperately needed for our nation, how can we expect 535 members of Congress to do so?" This is the question that haunted the agriculture leaders from across our country as we gathered in the Virginia suburbs just outside of Washington, DC.

Recognizing agriculture's indispensable need for labor and the bureaucratic nightmare our producers face as they struggle with the failed visa system that is inadequate to meet the market demands of our national food and fiber supply, we too attempted to swim through the political quagmire that has entrapped and figuratively drowned so many brave and strong souls before us. While some may have ulterior political motives, the agriculture industry knows this issue has brought together a wide group of reformers who, for economic reasons, understand we are doomed to defeat in the marketplace if we cannot develop a workable system.

Organizations like Texas Employers for Immigration Reform (TEIR) sprang up around the country in an attempt to bring the public together to focus on methods to solve this national enigma. The website of the Texas Association of Business led by former Texas State Representative Bill Hammond, a founding member of TEIR, describes the goal of this organization that attracted industry sectors such as manufacturing, construction, processors, and agriculture under one umbrella.

> TEIR is a coalition of Texas businesses fighting to fix a broken immigration system to assure real border security, restore law and order and provide access to a legal workforce that satisfies the needs of our growing economy.[42]

Other leaders based in Houston, Texas, like Norman Adams work through public and political circles to advance Texans for Sensible Immigration Policy. Conservative Republicans of Texas, led by Dr. Steven Hotze, recognize the myth that Latinos only vote Democrat and understand that Latinos are independent voters with shared conservative values. Brad Bailey, a Houston restaurateur, launched the Hard Work Clean Hands Initiative – a conservative alternative for immigration reform. Bailey served on the Texas Republican Party Platform committee and has been a tireless advocate and leader seeking reasonable solutions to these seemingly intractable dilemmas. Their efforts resulted in a major shift in the Republican Party of Texas Platform. The June 2012 convention resulted in amended and new language called the Texas Solution, which affirms that "mass deportation of these individuals would neither be equitable nor practical." This four-point plan also calls for a "national Temporary Worker Program…for periods of time when no US workers are currently available." Bailey continues a vigorous effort to reach consensus for a national solution.

Independent agriculture organizations have worked tirelessly to stoke Congress to at least recognize the unique needs of production agriculture. These organizations previously sought passage of the Ag Jobs bill. While this effort once showed momentum, it now sits idly by the wayside.

All Americans seem to agree our immigration system is broken. And if anyone cares to look, you would surely have to acknowledge how the guest labor force has enabled our economy to grow. Unfortunately, previous attempts to correct our failed immigration policy have faltered as there was not the overwhelming outcry to stop illegal immigration that has grown so vociferously during the last decade.

Well, the outcry is now here. Evidence is overwhelming that we have a violently dangerous and extremely porous border. Our future workforce is crucial to the economic well-being of all Americans. So why can't we fix this?

TRAPPED BY A FALSE CRISIS

O ur country has yet to be able to find workable solutions largely because of two factors: first, labor activists do not want a system that will allow for competition, and second, America cannot settle on the right course of action to deal with the estimated population working illegally in our country today.

American labor built this country. I should know—my father was one of them. He worked hard every single day of his blessed life, and he expected us to do the same, and I thank him for it (although it is doubtful I did at the time).

My father liked to work. When he went on vacation (which was seldom), you could sense on the way home he needed to go back to work to relax, not that work included relaxing in any way. When he was off his shift work at the glass factory, he worked at our small family cow-calf operation, worked at a family tree-trimming business, worked growing a garden, or studied in preparation to lead his men's Bible study class. When the glass plant closed down in 1984, a place where he worked rotating shifts for thirty-six years, our family opened up a retail plant nursery and landscaping business he operated the next twenty-plus years, six days a week. During the really busy spring planting months, it was six-and-a-half days a week. I believe he would have worked seven days a week, but he always found time for his church and family on Sundays.

I have said it before, but it bears repeating: every American who wants a job should have a job. Period.

Every American who wants a job should certainly have the opportunity to go seek a job before anyone outside our country has the opportunity to do so. That part is pretty simple and is something I believe in and is a philosophy I suspect shared by most Americans.

In thinking about labor and in wanting to ensure Americans are not displaced, this recent recession gives us some insight. Farming and ranching operations are not flooded with a domestic labor force. Even with the high unemployment rates across our nation due to the ramifications of this recession, we didn't see many of these unemployed lined up for agricultural, manual labor, or entry-level hospitality service jobs. In short, few relocated to the Texas Rio Grande Valley to pick grapefruit, to California to harvest strawberries, or to Washington State to help bring in the apple crop.

Agricultural labor is often paid above-minimum wage and, in many instances, well above minimum wage. I can tell you firsthand that operating sometimes fairly complex, and oftentimes very expensive equipment is no easy task. Algebraic math skills, using a rope, becoming familiar with using a welder, keeping small and large engines going, and factoring fertilizer rates and seed ratios takes more than just picking someone up on the side of the road to work. Not only is a certain skill set needed for a particular job, it is mostly done in very hot or cold weather where a fair amount of physical strength is needed, which adds yet another dimension to who will and can do this very important work to feed and clothe our country and now even supply some of our nation's energy.

Gary Black, Georgia commissioner of agriculture, has been an outspoken leader on the need for significant reforms to our failed immigration system and has testified before Congress for such. Black shared the Georgia Department of Agriculture's Report on Agriculture Labor[43] with all fifty agriculture commissioners, secretaries, and directors in February 2012.

The report conducted a thirty-six-question agriculture labor survey that was sent to over four thousand agriculture producers, processors, or related professions and had 813 respondents representing 87 percent of the counties in Georgia.

Among the significant findings are the following:

- All of the respondents reported paying full-time and part-time workers at or above the federal minimum wage.
- In it, 26 percent of respondents reported a loss of income due to the lack of available workers.
- They cited burdensome and cumbersome H2A visa requirements for ag labor.

This data paints a clear picture of the importance of a reliable labor force and the role guest labor has played in meeting the needs of our economy. Yet our nation's history has too many examples where organized labor is not thrilled about a system that allows for too many people to be able to come into our country and work. All of us need to step away from the plate, breathe deeply, and consider the thoughts of a leading investor in our country.

AVOIDING CRISIS

BlackRock chief equity strategist Bob Doll was interviewed by James Freeman in the June 4, 2011, edition of the *Wall Street Journal*. BlackRock was handling *only* about $3.6 trillion at the time![44] In the article, which discussed the future of the US economy, Doll cited projected population growth rates in the United States, Europe, and Japan. America was the only nation with a projected positive population growth rate. Doll, with substantial money on the line, emphatically explained how population growth impacts a nation's economy:

> "The long-term growth rate of any economy is the product of the change in the size of the work force multiplied by the productivity of the work force." Productivity is very hard to predict, he reports, but demographics is easy. "You count noses." And that tally shows a very healthy America.[45]

It is important to note that investment strategist Doll included both high immigration rates and higher fertility rates as the factors positioning our population growth rate to exceed the competition.

TECHNOLOGY CAN HELP

Do you have a credit card, debit card, or prepaid card you use to pay your bills? If not, you are part of the 5.6 percent of American consumers who are like my wife and would rather pay cash or write a check. Almost 90 percent of US consumers have a cell phone of some sort.[46] We can now pay our bills with our credit cards on our mobile phones, but not while driving, right? Right.

My point is this: almost everyone in this country has used an electronic convenience card and most likely on a daily basis. Surely, technology has advanced enough to deliver the appropriate tools to help us know who is coming in and out of our country legally, who is working legally, and how to stop the underground economies that arise from an illegal population. These black market economies tax all of us who are complying with the laws of the United States.

This can be done in a way that doesn't make "Big Brother" stronger and empower government.

Maybe we should put it out for bid to American Express, MasterCard, Visa, Discover, or Diners Club? They seem to be able to keep track of who owes which business what amount of money and, it appears, are pretty quick to point out fraud and shut down unauthorized or suspicious use of credit cards.

A LARGER CRISIS LOOMS

Americans enjoy the safest, most affordable, and reliable food supply in the world thanks to our nation's farmers and ranchers. Want evidence? According to the US Department of Agriculture, in 2011 Americans spent 6.7 percent of total household expenditures for food consumed at home, the lowest percentage of any country. For comparison, it was 9.4 percent in the United Kingdom, 21.3 percent in China, and 22.7 percent in Mexico.[47] In all, Americans spent a little less than 10 percent of our disposable income on food.[48]

Innovation, creativity, and solid research have been the basis of the productivity that continues to lead the world today. Considering many countries do not have the same labor and environmental standards as we do, I want a domestic food supply. Approximately 83% of the food we eat in America is from food produced in America, and I'd like to keep it that way.[49]

We do not like being dependent on foreign oil. We must not, we cannot, become dependent on foreign food. Food security is fundamental to national security. Tanks can't run and planes cannot fly on empty fuel tanks; soldiers, sailors, airmen, and marines cannot fight on empty stomachs. In fact, it was the Department of Defense who initially called for the National School Lunch program because too many young men entering military service during World War II were malnourished and in no condition to endure the rigorous training and battlefield conditions that awaited them. America can, and yes, did do better. Unfortunately and ironically, too many volunteers in our nation's military today are overweight. The pendulum has swung.

AMNESTY HAS BEEN TRIED IN THIS COUNTRY—IT FAILED

A dissertation is not needed to verify the Immigration Reform and Control Act of 1986 failed. Why would we be discussing what to do with 11 to 20 million people who entered our country illegally if the 1986 amnesty effort was successful?

To get an even clearer picture of the failures of previous immigration reforms, one should consider the debate surrounding the Immigration and Naturalization Act of 1965. As with most major pieces of legislation, there have been many assertions presented as facts, but the real and final judgment should be based on the outcome of implementation.

In efforts to distract from the naysayers of the bill, Congress assured the American people that the legislation would have little effect on the immigration patterns, and its influence would be minimal. Well, this wasn't the first time, or the last, Congress missed the boat. The result of the legislation: increased illegal immigration from Latin America and waves of new immigrants from other areas of the world.[50]

Signing the 1965 act into law, our nation's thirty-sixth President, Lyndon Baines Johnson, commented this "is not a revolutionary bill. It does not affect the lives of millions…It will not reshape the structure of our daily lives or add importantly to either our wealth or our power."[51]

A summation of the act's impact is as follows:

> All told, in the three decades following passage of the Immigration and Naturalization Act of 1965, more than 18 million legal immigrants entered the United States, more than three times the number admitted over the preceding 30 years.[52]

Maybe when President Johnson said "It does not affect the lives of millions," what he meant was it wouldn't in a single year. This math error reminds us of the miscalculations surrounding Medicare, right? Any wonder why people all over the country are more than a little nervous about what will be the impact on costs and taxes of the Affordable Health Care for America Act, a.k.a. Obamacare. Okay, I won't go there.

Let's go back to one of my favorite quotes from Dr. Walter Williams, "Policy intentions and policy effects often bear no relationship to one another."[53] After reading the quote from President Johnson and my own experiences as a Texas state legislator, I can only surmise the following:

> Policy *analysis* and policy *outcomes* often bear no relationship to one another.

I guess the real point here is there is no wonder Congress has consistently low approval ratings. You just need to get it right some of the time.

DON'T CONFUSE THE PAST WITH THE PRESENT

Now, as any child who has been educated in this country can readily attest, we are a nation of immigrants. It began at Plymouth Rock. Some came through Ellis Island. Some came through Galveston Island. Many did not come through a formal or legal system of immigration at all, but that was then.

My great-grandpa Jerry was said to be a lad when he left his home country of Ireland. No one in the family knows where he was from, what part of Ireland he called home, or why he left. No one has ever provided an ounce of evidence about the origins of Grandpa Jerry nor have we traveled the oceans to trace his trail. All that is told is young Jerry Staples signed up to work on a ship setting sail for America, agreeing to work aboard for his passage fare.

Once aboard, the captain and crew had different plans. The course they charted for young Jerry was one of indentured servitude—they made a slave of him. The story does not tell of the hardships aboard the vessel, of the times he endured sufferings, or of his mental state of mind. What we were told time and again is that young Jerry saw the shores of the United States, and that was all he needed. He lunged overboard, diving headfirst into the choppy waters, and swam vigorously with every muscle in his body and breath in his lungs until he ultimately washed ashore, exhausted. Jerry would have been my great-grandfather whom I never knew. While this is told to be a factual account, I will likely never be able to determine the veracity of this piece of my family's story. But I have passed this narrative down to my children as a reminder to them of the sacrifices made to achieve the opportunities held within America's shores.

While we all acknowledge we are a nation of immigrants with a storied past, our security, our economy, and our future demand we be a country of legal immigration today, and we allow all who come under our rules the opportunity to live fully and freely the American dream. For some, the dream takes time to develop. For others, the dream matures in their lifetime. For others, it awaits the next generation.

We in this generation have an obligation and duty to solve our current dilemma. It weighs on both the conscience of our country and the strength of our economy. For too long, our approach to dealing with illegal immigration has been a wink-and-nod policy that has proliferated into national tension that divides rather than unites us.

SOME ISSUES GET HIJACKED AND DETER US FROM THE GOAL

The Development, Relief, and Education for Alien Minors Act (DREAM Act) seeks to offer a pathway to citizenship for minors who came illegally into our country under the age of sixteen and meet certain requirements, including living in the USA for at least five years and graduating from high school, entering college, or serving in the military for a certain period of time.

Opponents vehemently call this amnesty and an incentive to come to the country illegally. Proponents argue it is not amnesty because certain and rigorous criteria must be met prior to benefitting from the act.

During the Republican presidential primary debates in the fall of 2011, House Bill 1403 passed by the Texas Legislature in 2001 was labeled the Texas DREAM Act. This legislation, with no opposing testimony in committee, was passed by an overwhelmingly conservative body of legislators with unanimous approval in the Senate and only four dissenting votes in the House. It would allow a minor who was in the state illegally to pay in-state tuition under certain specific conditions: he or she went to school for three years in Texas, graduated from high school, and was applying for citizenship.

Decisions, good or bad, should be viewed in the prism of circumstances and time in which they were made. I might point out it was widely assumed when HB 1403 was passed (incorrectly so) that the federal government would require those few who did participate to correct their status. The feds failed again.

Let me assure you, at the time of passage, House Bill 1403 had nothing to do with immigration but everything to do with education. It was debated in the *education* committees. Nowhere on anyone's radar screen was this bill contemplated to be, as described in the Republican debates, an incentive to migrate into this country illegally. If it had been, I can say with certainty it would not have passed.

As discussions on the DREAM Act churned, immigration became a litmus test for many conservatives. The perception was any proposal that proposed any action other than automatic and swift deportation was deemed unacceptable and un-American. There was no debating the issue. HB 1403 was morphed into the federal act and deemed by a majority of Republican primary voters throughout the country as wrong, wrong, wrong and soft, soft, soft on immigration. Realizing increased education attainment benefits all of society and not just the one receiving it, the Texas Legislature was attempting to improve conditions and assumed anyone participating in HB 1403 would either follow our federal laws on citizenship or have been required to return to their country of origin. If the bill were introduced in Texas today under the current environment, it most likely would not pass.

What is wrong with HB 1403 now and what is wrong with the DREAM Act is that these proposals, and others like them, are being pushed as isolated immigration reform bills without correcting the real onslaught of problems associated with porous international borders, or dealing with the millions who are in the country illegally today. Texans, as well as all Americans, are looking for a way to *allow* for *legal* immigration and to *stop* illegal immigration.

Taking partial action on these types of initiatives says we are not serious about the bigger predicament, and believe me, Americans are serious. We do need to have the debate about children who grew up here, about the millions here illegally, about those who serve in the

United States military, about the needs of our workforce, and about the cover given criminal organizations when we have a porous border, but we must not give in to partial solutions that perpetuate this system that fails both citizen and noncitizen alike. We must not lose sight of the big picture here: porous border, inadequate workforce, failed immigration policies; a broad view demonstrates these are tied together, and any proposal that purports to solve one without addressing the others fails and only makes matters worse, not better.

A TEXAS TAKE

RAISE YOUR RIGHT HAND AND REPEAT AFTER ME

The headquarters of the Texas Department of Agriculture is in the Stephen. F. Austin State Office Building, just two blocks north of the State Capitol in Austin.

Our agency has around 650 full-time employees and is housed on three floors of the eleven-story building. When not traveling, I usually arrive early before it's crowded and will occasionally find myself riding the elevator up to the top floor with a man named Neil who works in our Administrative Services Division. Two things really stand out about Neil. First, with his build, he could be mistaken for an offensive tackle, and he has a distinctively non-Texan accent.

The morning of April 26, 2011, was just like any other for me, but as I rode the elevator with Neil, I knew that day was special for him. Neil's dress code is normally business casual, but this morning he was dressed in a suit and tie.

"Neil, what's the occasion?" I asked.

He replied with his heavy English accent, "Today, I am taking the oath to become an American citizen."

I changed my plans for that day and attended the ceremony to watch Neil swear to uphold the Constitution of the United States of America. Almost 1,000 other people from 105 countries across the globe took the oath in that one ceremony. It was overwhelming and humbling to literally see the unity, patriotism, and pride shared by the new citizens and their families.

Later, I learned Sowjayna Katpalli and Hong Su, two other TDA employees, had become American citizens a few months earlier. My next door neighbors, David and Carolina Dominguez, both immigrated and became United States citizens through the naturalizatoin process. They worked while attending college and teach in public schools today.

I highly recommend every native-born American to attend a naturalization ceremony. It is an emotional experience to witness the hopes and dreams of people who have come to our country seeking a better life. Some may have been seeking freedom from religious persecution as did many who colonized America, others may be seeking economic liberty, and perhaps others are fulfilling a longing for the adventure of a new start.

For those of us born in America, we didn't have a choice to make, and if you are like most Americans, you have never considered the possibility of citizenship in another country. Why go elsewhere when you are already a part of the best?

I thank God I was born an American. I thank God he has preserved our republic throughout the last two hundred-plus years and pray that he will in the future as well.

Each generation of Americans has a choice to make in regard to what the next generation will inherit. I want to continue to be a country where people will want to stand up in a room of thousands, raise their right hand, and willingly choose to join us as American citizens.

MONUMENTS REPRESENT OUR PAST, PEOPLE REPRESENT OUR FUTURE

Jan and I were leaving an event in Washington, DC, that had taken place on the National Mall, and we were holding hands as we were walking slowly back to our hotel, taking in the sights. We both love history and enjoy experiencing it together.

From all directions we could see monuments representing our nation's rich heritage. There are shrines to heroic figures whose patriotic dreams shaped our country and bold declarations capturing the spirit of Americans etched into the side of buildings.

As we stopped and soaked in the majesty of the moment and gazed at these fabulous tributes with their entire splendor, we knew they paled in comparison to the meaning that is represented by a new generation of Americans with new responsibilities to carry forward what these resolute edifices represented. Our people are our greatest and strongest asset.

IT ALL STARTS AND ENDS WITH THE LAND

Why is a state commissioner of agriculture involved in border security?

For Texans, that is like asking "Why does a horse run or a cow have horns?" Non-Texans may need a little more interpretation.

Why doesn't a quarterback just hand off the ball? Why does he scramble, throw the ball, and even sometimes catch a pass? He does these things to help his team win. He does whatever it takes to accomplish the team goals.

Texans demand action, not words. They want results, not rhetoric. Whether in business or serving as an elected official, my philosophy is when someone comes to you with a problem, you don't look at them, nod, and grimace with concern then go on about your way. This too often describes the Washington way—not the Texas way.

In Texas, as in many states, you make sure the dilemma is sufficiently decided. If the problem doesn't get resolved the first time, you keep pushing, pulling, and leveraging until you start to see the desired results. Throwing hands up in despair is unacceptable. You keep working until you get it right.

When a rancher looks in your eyes with tears welling up in his, you give him your full attention. He tells you his family settled the border and tamed the land he lives on today; nevertheless, he is fearfully aware of the constant risk that his family could fall prey to the violence of the drug trafficking that occurs regularly along the border and become yet another kidnap victim or worse. When a tough, independent, hard-as-nails rancher says help is needed, action is required.

To the many families who have scratched a living out of the land, encroachments of any kind are simply not tolerated. The land defines you; there is an emotional bond that is unbreakable. The parts of the US Constitution that you think about regularly are the Fifth and Fourteenth Amendments that protect us from being deprived of life, liberty, and *property*. Spillover violence is a tremendous threat to all three. You also draw comfort in knowing the Second Ammendment allows you to protect the Fifth and Fourteenth.

THE PROBLEMS GROW

I had heard of sporadic problems in Mexico for years. I chaired the Texas Senate Committee on Transportation and Homeland Security during the Seventy-Eighth Legislature. We held a hearing in the McAllen area in 2004, and the local committee host asked to take our delegation into Reynosa for the evening meal. My committee director and general counsel advised me the US State Department had issued a travel advisory urging Americans not to travel into that part of Mexico. Our state homeland security officials confirmed the state department's concerns and advice were legitimate and advised us to heed the warning. As chair of the committee, I was responsible for the lives of thirty or so people who would be making the evening excursion. It would have been a short low-key trip, and some pressured my staff to convince or lobby me to take the group as a matter of protocol. My decision was simple. How could I face the family of anyone who might possibly be injured when our own state department advised against the trip? We did not go.

The problem has only gotten worse with time. The horrendous violence occurring in the northern Mexican states has been well chronicled in the news. The kidnappings, drive-by shootings, headless bodies displayed in public venues, mass graves, and lifeless figures left in the streets are not a Hollywood movie script. They are reality.

These tragedies are the results of warring drug cartels fighting for turf and market share. They are intentionally making victims of honest Mexican citizens who just want to live their lives, raise their families, and work in their communities. The cartels are intentionally making victims of Texas farmers, ranchers, and landowners by systematically deploying a strategy to make Texas a stronghold in their black market expansion.

My reelection as our state's agriculture commissioner was ramping up for the 2010 election. I had heard the stories of spillover violence and how it was making victims of Texas farmers and ranchers. I had seen the pictures of dead bodies scattered along Texas ranches. Some landowners wanted me to go public with the stories that had been brought to me and raise awareness of their cause. Some said it would make "one helluva campaign" platform to run on. The issue was real. The problem was getting worse. The resources the local, state, and federal law enforcement authorities needed to protect landowners, while increased from previous years, were clearly insufficient, and Washington was not delivering reinforcements. I immediately started digging in, gathering information, and developing solutions but chose not to act publicly because anything released during the height of a campaign would likely be dismissed as posturing. My staff had direction to do everything possible to work with law enforcement officials to ensure the safety and property of the landowners were protected. We all knew more would be needed to bring a resolution.

TIMING IS KEY

Campaigns are a thrill to me. Debating the issues of our day, listening to the people who are the backbone of our state and country, and engaging in a system that allows a humble country boy raised on a farm by God-fearing, hardworking, honest, and loving parents with limited means to serve as a mayor pro tem, state representative, state senator and a statewide elected official means the promise of America is very much alive. To me, it also means the promise is very much worth protecting, preserving, and passing along to our children and grandchildren so they can engage in the pursuit of happiness.

Nothing is more despicable in a campaign than for the candidate or his team to contrive a problem to convince the public of the candidate's leadership or use a disaster for political gain. As a youngster, I remember hearing of an East Texas state representative staging a shooting of himself to help in his bid to seek higher office.

The tales of "Who Shot Mike Martin?" were well-chronicled by Dan Balz in the *Washington Post*. Unfortunately for Texas, the story found a wide circulation, including a reprint of Balz's story in the *Spokesman-Review* in Spokane, WA.[54]

Things didn't go well for the one-term state representative when his first cousin spilled the beans and confessed to helping stage the whole event to advance Martin's political career. If it looks like a duck, walks like a duck, quacks like a duck...it must be a duck. Martin laid an egg on this one.

While the atrocities against our landowners were and are real, making this a campaign issue, I feared, would have been met by those we most urgently needed turning a deaf ear to the problems and the crisis. I waited until my reelection campaign was over to step up and publicly engage on the issue. Little did I know, the deafness was already impermeable.

HOW SAFE IS THE BORDER? JUST THE FACTS

For those of us in business, the facts are the facts. You analyze and understand the weaknesses in the methodologies and resources used to develop the information, but once you evaluate the data, the facts are the facts.

Unfortunately, the facts are not the facts when it comes to our federal government. Politics guide the numbers and the facts. Although they know the Federal Bureau of Investigation statistics leave out a host of crimes committed by cartels, President Obama and Secretary Janet Napolitano cite improving crime statistics in cities along the border.

Consciously misapplying the numbers at a time when landowners are coming forward with the ongoing saga of appalling tragedies that are occurring on their land only emboldens the enemy and sacrifices our sovereignty. Bullet holes don't lie! Dead bodies tell a powerful story! I refuse to accept a tolerance level for violence that ignores the pleas of our people as they are being chased from their land. More must be done when our liberties are at stake.

In an effort to bring attention to the reality about the insecure border, the Texas Department of Agriculture created www.ProtectYourTexasBorder.com.

With an existing small but talented staff, and a video camera, and by paying $22.99 per year for a website name, a voice was born. The Protect Your Texas Border website would allow Texas farmers and ranchers who live and work along the border and the corridors of cartel trafficking operations to tell their story firsthand. People will believe farmers and ranchers relaying the events that occur on their own property, right? Wrong.

DEFENDING THE EVIDENCE, DEFENDING THE LANDOWNER

Soon after ProtectYourTexasBorder.com went live, Texas State Senator Jose Rodriquez (D), El Paso, wrote a demand letter insisting I pull down the site.

US Representative Sylvester Reyes (D), El Paso, Texas, was quoted in the *Texas Tribune* as saying "Our state is facing a $27 billion budget crisis, and our state leaders are wasting scarce tax dollars to support a platform that portrays rural Texas like rural Afghanistan."[55]

I was summoned to face the Texas Democratic Caucus and answer for my alleged insensitivity and inappropriate use of state resources. However, in laying out the case of the tragedies that were occurring to our mutual constituents, I found the number of complainers was very limited. Many knew and understood what I discovered; lives are at stake, and the issues are not to be glossed over.

ProtectYourTexasBorder.com will be disabled only when the violence and invasion stops—when Texans no longer fear being chased off their land, and they can use and enjoy their private property as is protected under our United States Constitution. Landowners cannot be abandoned and left to live in fear, especially on their own property.

TAKING ACTION TO PROTECT LANDOWNERS ISN'T NEW

Responding to crises on the border isn't new for Texans. It happened frequently during the later part of the nineteenth century by dispatching men on horseback, and unfortunately, it occurred in the later part of the twentieth century as well, long before the current difficulties landowners are now experiencing.

A July 1997 headline in the *New York Times* read "The Drug Lords of Maverick County." The article details the enormous increase in drug trafficking in this rural area. It cites, "US and local law enforcement agencies are aware that the ranchers in once-tranquil Maverick County, Tex., are under siege."

Tony Castaneda, chief of the Eagle Pass Police, says, "I'm uneasy myself, and I'm trained for this. They're haulin' drugs just down from my house. I even carry a .38 to mow my lawn, but those guys are carrying assault rifles."[56]

Disgusted with headlines highlighting the brazenness of drug cartels crossing the river and trampling through Maverick County, James Francis of Dallas wanted action. Francis chaired the Public Safety Commission that governs the Texas Department of Public Safety. He recalls reaching out to General Barry McCaffrey, head of a joint task force created to combat the increasing illegal narcotic trade invading America, and officially requested federal assistance to stop, as he put it, the "lawlessness in Maverick County and to put an end to the bandits who were running rampant." To his dismay, McCaffrey declined the request, referencing the lack of resources and the commitment to ongoing work in California.

Francis, through the colonel of the Texas DPS, James Wilson, refused to abandon a Texas county and landowners to seedy and criminal elements. They knew what was needed was a definitive "show of force," according to Francis.

With very little notice, Colonel Wilson redirected 130 state troopers and seventy highway patrol cars to this Texas border county. When challenged about how long the Texas DPS was going to continue this "diversion" of assets to this community, Francis replied with unwavering resolve, "As long as necessary." Francis recalls that with the aggressive presence of Texas DPS troopers, the violence subsided, and the effort was able to be disbanded in about three months time.[57]

Meeting force with a greater and determined force wins.

TEXAS ROUNDUP

To be clear, border security resources under both President George W. Bush and President Barack Obama have increased. There are more border patrol agents and more equipment. Congress authorized the border fence. People living along the border wish it were as simple as a fence, but they know it is not. People who care about the constitutional protections of private property owner rights wish neither the violence nor the fence harmed them, but they do.

In the absence of adequate federal support, Governor Rick Perry and other state leaders focused on the need to protect our citizens and stem the flow of illegal drugs and weapons being used against our law enforcement officials.

TEXANS TAKE ACTION

Not enough can be said about the gallant efforts of our federal, state, and local law enforcement officials who put their lives on the line to protect our people and defend our country. Their ongoing efforts, despite Washington's politically motivated denials, are the only backstop that has kept the cartels from overtaking our border regions.

BOOTS ON THE GROUND

I first met Steve McCraw around 2005 when I was chair of the Texas Senate Committee on Transportation and Homeland Security. Some may ponder what transportation and homeland security have to do with one another. Well, we are efficient in Texas. We do what we have to do.

Steve, a native of El Paso, started his law enforcement career with the Texas Department of Public Safety in 1977. After spending twenty-one years with the FBI where his assignments included unit chief of an Organized Crime Unit, director of a Foreign Terrorism Tracking Task Force after 9/11, special agent in charge of the San Antonio Field Division, and assistant director for the Office of Intelligence and the Inspection Division in Washington, DC, McCraw moved back home to serve the state of Texas. He is now director of the Texas Department of Public Safety.[58]

McCraw and I both attended a security briefing at CIA headquarters in Langley, Virginia, several years ago. There we met with homeland security officials and elected leaders from throughout the nation who were playing a role in security matters. The major theme of the conference was how the barriers to communication were broken after September 11.

Our national security agencies understood they must engage in a greater sharing of information to save American lives and to combat terror at home and abroad. Steve's role in developing a new information-sharing system while he was with the FBI was referenced during that conference. He certainly brought that expertise home to Texas and has been successful in using it.

Among the initiatives developed under McCraw's leadership, the Texas Fusion Center works around the clock with federal, state, regional, and local law enforcement as well as the public to receive and analyze data and determine threat levels.

The Border Security Operations Center is responsible for centralizing information related to crime along the Texas-Mexico border. It is located at DPS headquarters but works with the dozens and dozens of local, state, and federal law enforcement agencies participating in Operation Border Star.

There are six Joint Operations Intelligence Centers, one located in each of the border security sectors that share information and make operational decisions. They are a nerve center for all law enforcement agencies operating in the sector.

These are just a few of the tools that are working together for a safer Texas and America. Governor Rick Perry continues to put the people in place, and he and the members of the Texas Legislature, led by Lieutenant Governor David Dewhurst and Speaker Joe Straus, former Senator Steve Ogden, Senator Tommy Williams, Senator Craig Estes, and Representative Jim Pitts have dedicated millions of dollars in order to combat this threat emanating from an international source.

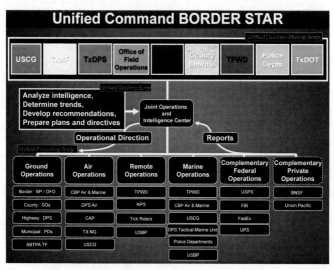

Source: Texas Department of Public Safety

THE GAME PLAN

In 2006, Operation Linebacker was launched, coordinating eighteen Texas border (or near border) sheriffs to combat Mexican cartels smuggling in their counties. This initiative grew and was later expanded into Operation Border Star, which brought together a combination of talent with forces from US Customs and Border Patrol, sixty-five police departments, fifty-three border and coastal county law enforcement agencies, the Texas Parks and Wildlife Department, Texas Military Forces, US Coast Guard, and the Texas Department of Public Safety.

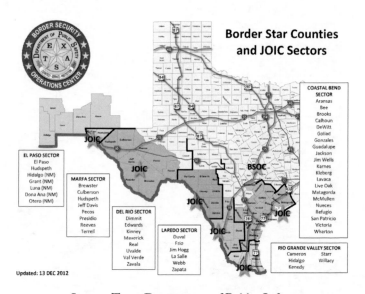

Source: Texas Department of Public Safety

From 2006 to 2011, Operation Border Star denied the cartels over $8.4 billion in drug profits. The combined efforts of the multiple crime-fighting agencies prevented the distribution and use of the following illegal substances to cities all across America:

- 6.9 million pounds of marijuana
- 73,428 pounds of cocaine
- 1,737 pounds of heroin
- 5,987 pounds of methamphetamine

In the course of their work, local and state officers turned over 56,041 suspected illegal aliens to the US Border Patrol. [59]

SMILE FOR THE CAMERA

Operation Drawbridge is in effect today. This initiative strategically places what are essentially "game" cameras like those used by outdoorsmen, equipped with a built-in cell phone, along suspected drug routes, providing constant, real-time monitoring of the border by the Texas Fusion Center. Suspicious activity is conveyed immediately to the local Border Patrol, the sheriff's office, other law enforcement, and the landowner hosting the camera.[60] Many of these photos can be seen on www.protectyourtexasborder.com.

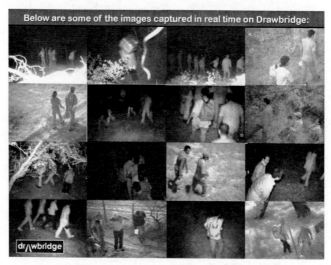

Source: Texas Department of Public Safety

Cooperative landowners are a key component of the ability to implement Drawbridge, and most have been eager participants, with some limited resistance due to fear of retaliation. DPS personnel introduced the camera strategy to me during a landowner listening session I conducted in the Valley. Immediately recognizing the tremendous benefit to the property owner and law enforcement efforts of this relatively low-cost technology, my team reached out to our land steward organizations whose members are constantly plagued by an insecure and dangerous border. Texas Farm Bureau, Texas & Southwestern Cattle Raisers Association, Texas Wildlife Association, and South Texans Property Rights Association quickly came together and learned about the strategy and began discreetly disseminating the information to their members. Determining where to place the cameras is pretty simple: follow the trails that have been created by the volume of illegal activity trampling across these landowners' private property. The results of this organized effort have been phenomenal.

"Operation Drawbridge provides undeniable photographic proof that private landowners are constantly dealing with the dangers of deadly drug cartels and the impact of illegal human trafficking" was my lead quote in a June 21, 2012, press release issued by the Texas Department of Agriculture recognizing the success of our law enforcement officers. We were quick to compliment and thank the Texas Department of Public Safety, US Border Patrol, and Texas Border sheriffs on this surveillance initiative that has not only illustrated the effectiveness of leveraging technology and law enforcement partnerships but clearly depicts the dangers that occur on a daily basis.

Operation Drawbridge has resulted in the apprehension of more than two thousand individuals and more than five tons of narcotics just from January to June 2012, this with only 250 cameras in place to cover 1,241 miles of Texas-Mexico border. All government initiatives should be envious of results like this. That's why I utilized $225,000 from agency efficiency savings in late 2012 to transfer to DPS so they could double the number of cameras in Operation Drawbridge.

One of the landowner organizations had a picture of a well-worn trail on the cover of their membership magazine demonstrating South Texas private lands have become access routes taking illegal substances all across America. The sentiments of the landowners were summed up with this statement.

"This effort and use of technology is very timely and very much appreciated," said Texas Wildlife Association President Glen Webb. "We know many landowners within one hundred miles or more of the border who are arming employees for their own protection. In some cases, families are forced to self-impose curfews to avoid leaving their houses at night, which has ultimately led many families to make the decision to move off their own ranches and out of their homes."[61]

GRIT ON THE RANGE AND IN THE AIR

Flying at night over the remote areas of our southern border in a Texas Department of Public Safety helicopter is something all Americans should experience. It gives an unparalleled perspective of the daunting challenge to secure the border.

Daylight is gone. The stars are high in the sky, sheltered by thin layers of clouds. The captain and his copilot, armed with sidearms and with additional ordinance on board, yell "Clear!" as they begin the rotors that will lift us to our point of observation 1,500 feet above the scrub brush that covers the sparsely populated rural stretches of the Rio Grande. The isolated and dimly lit landing pad disappears below as we take flight to become the eyes in the air for the boots on the ground.

It is a Texas Ranger recon mission, a coordinated crime-stopping machine that incorporates multiple agencies to deter those who seek to come into our country illegally, regardless of the trespassers' ultimate objective. The members of the recon team don't care about taking credit or blame. It is not their job to determine motives or consequences. Their job is to defend the border and protect the people of the United States of America, and they do an amazing job with the resources they have.

Below, you can see the ground personnel from the forward-looking infrared (FLIR) cameras on board the aircraft. FLIR uses imaging technology that senses infrared radiation. This captures the Border Patrol and other reconnaissance members on the ground as they move in a sweeping motion with flashlights, scouting out a group of men who illegally crossed the border and are now hiding in the brush. The suspects cannot escape the airborne sentinel prowling overhead.

While aboard a flight myself, I saw on the observation screen, and I overheard the chatter from the pilot to the ground unit below: *Kilo 24, proceed ten yards to your 12 o'clock... Kilo 24, the subject is three yards to your 9 o'clock... Kilo 24, the subject is directly beneath you!*

The subject complies with the officer's demands to lie on the ground with his hands above his head. The fierce resolve coupled with technological superiority enabled the successful mission despite the obscurity of the late evening hours.

Another situation doesn't end so quickly as the subject flees. The chase is on.

My fly along was comparatively uneventful, but DPS documents reveal the seriousness of the crimes, the increasing frequency with which they occur, and the danger our officers face.

SPLASHDOWN 101

Better than any Hollywood version, drug cartel members offer dynamic filming opportunities when they evade our law enforcement officers and drive their drug-laden vehicles directly into the Rio Grande in order to escape capture. Since 2009, splashdowns (as they are called) have occurred sixty-five times.[62]

A stolen pickup truck speeds down the road. Law enforcement officers respond. The truck picks up speed; blue and red lights flash and sirens wail as our officers accept the challenge, and the chase begins. Overhead, DPS helicopters provide a spotlight and navigational support for the teams on the ground. With the Rio Grande River quickly approaching and the road being traveled a dead end, the casual observer would think the chase would soon be over. Not so.

Without a tap of the brakes, the driver sails between the narrow banks of the river, plunging the stolen auto into the otherwise calm stream of the Rio Grande that will later be used to water a farmer's field.

Border Patrol, state DPS, local sheriff's deputies, and city police stand helplessly along the US banks of the Rio Grande as they watch two boats already launched from the Mexican side speed toward the dog-paddling driver of the vehicle and the tightly wrapped bags of dope floating nearby. As the cartel members gather their load, US law enforcement watch, knowing this scene will be repeated many times.

Here is the challenge, the weakness our officers face and how they know the scene will be repeated. The international border provides an escape route. There is a significant lack of coordination between Mexico and the United States. Our law enforcement is hamstrung and prohibited from fully engaging with offenders. Our limited law enforcement resources leave gaps and unattended, open holes.

USING ALL THE TOOLS

After graduating from college, I bought my first house inside the city limits of Palestine. It was a fixer-upper, but luckily, my friend Jackie Gragg's father, Jack Lockey, lived across the street. For eighty years, Mr. Lockey had collected a massive home repair toolbox—everything you could possibly imagine. Practically every time I needed to make a repair, Mr. Lockey would skeptically watch me for a few minutes and then walk across the street to offer just the right tool. I would try to make the repairs with the limited tools I had, but without the right resources, I usually wasted time and often created even more damage. When Mr. Lockey showed up with the right tool and I properly used it, the repair effort was much more successful.

It doesn't take long to realize that when the correct tools are properly utilized, you can solve any problem. It also doesn't take long to understand that you can't turn a screw with a hammer, and it's near impossible to drive a nail with a wrench. You must have a diverse set of tools to meet the challenges you will encounter.

Our federal government needs to realize that our border is broken. It is the responsibility of our leaders in Washington to ensure our law enforcement agents are properly equipped to repair it. Further, it is Washington's responsibility to ensure *all* tools are available and used to make sure the job is done correctly. Concentrating law enforcement only in urban areas or only along the

California border doesn't fix the problem. We need more agents in rural areas, more technology to bridge the gaps, a workable immigration system, and a way to legally move goods and people.

Article IV, Section IV of the United States Constitution, bears repeating:

> The United States shall guarantee to every State in this Union a Republican Form of Government, *and shall protect each of them against Invasion; and on Application of the Legislature, or of the Executive* (when the Legislature cannot be convened) *against domestic violence.*

Why is it so hard for some officials to understand that a failure to accomplish protection is, well, unconstitutional? You can call it domestic violence; we call it invasion of our property. By anyone's definition, protection is required to be provided by our federal government. Protection must be accomplished, not discussed.

The irony is that our federal government must agree with part of our plea; otherwise, why is federal law enforcement scattered along the border in such vast numbers today? As of April 9, 2011, one month before President Obama made his famous, but audaciously condescending, speech at the Chamizal National Memorial in El Paso about the security of our border, US Department of Homeland Security reported a total of 20,745 border patrol agents up from the 17,499 agents just four months before he took office. Why would 85% of the agents be stationed along the southwest border with Mexico if there wasn't a crisis needing to be fully resolved?[63]

What is the size of force necessary to restore the peace? History offers us a glimpse.

The Mexican Expedition of 1916 was a US military exercise in response to a surprise attack by Pancho Villa on the town of Columbus, New Mexico. President Woodrow Wilson sent between 75,000 and 150,000 troops to defeat the opposing force and protect our citizens.[64]

There is a problem, and the federal government acknowledges the problem...to a point. It is time we use all our tools to stop the problem.

Going back to the lessons of World War II, when my father-in-law passed away, we read through his army discharge papers to prepare for his eulogy. He never talked much about his military service during World War II, but the United States Army discharge papers provided the details.

Private First Class Frank Wendel, who received the Purple Heart, Marksmanship, and Good Conduct medals, was not idle during his military service. The army confirmed he was engaged in five major battles during WWII: Normandy, Northern France, Central Europe, Ardennes, and Rhineland.

What was even more amazing was that he was enlisted for less than three years. My wife Jan and I were having dinner with retired General Barry McCaffrey and Major General Robert Scales one evening shortly after the services honoring "Papa's" life, and I expressed my astonishment that all the major battles he fought occurred in less than three years. General Scales leaned forward and politely but commandingly said, "Commissioner, he did all that in less than ten months!"

Here's the lesson: Private Wendel served in five major engagements in less than ten months because the Allied forces were fighting with everything they had. Our leaders were focused, and our troops were dedicated. Losing, tying, or playing tag was not an option. Winning decisively was the commitment from everyone in American uniform. The only solution was defeating the enemy, no matter the cost.

I know the circumstances are different, I know the enemy was more defined in WWII, and I am not by any means suggesting we militarize our southern border (at this point in time) because we have not yet used all our tools. I am convinced, however, that if we have the will to protect and defend the sovereignty of the United States of America from the terror being spread by these transnational criminal organizations, we can accomplish our goal. And we must. *Tolerance of these encroachments is acceptance.* Americans should reject any such notion.

A SIX-STAR REPORT

If our federal officials won't believe the people who provide us with the safest, most affordable, and most abundant food and fiber supply in the world, maybe they will believe patriots who have dedicated their lives to fighting for liberty and protecting and defending borders all over the globe.

Directing even more state resources to provide another tool to fix this federal problem, in 2011, the Texas Legislature directed the Department of Agriculture, along with the Texas Department of Public Safety, to conduct an analysis of the border and answer, essentially, these two questions: is the Texas border under attack, and if so, what do we need to do about it?

In September 2011, TDA and the Texas Department of Public Safety released "Texas Border Security: A Strategic Military Assessment" prepared by General Barry R. McCaffrey (Ret) and Major General Robert H. Scales (Ret).

General McCaffrey has a legacy of service to his country and a reputation as a diplomat and a military strategist. Upon his retirement from active duty, General McCaffrey was the most highly decorated four-star general in the US Army. In 1996, he was unanimously confirmed by the US Senate to serve as a member of the President's Cabinet and the National Security Council for drug-related issues. In this position, he coordinated the $19 billion federal drug control budget and developed the US National Drug Control Strategy.

Major General (Dr.) Robert H. Scales is a respected authority on land warfare. Major General Scales served more than thirty years in the army, earned the prestigious Silver Star, and served in command and staff positions in the United States, Germany, and Korea, ending his military career as commandant of the United States Army War College. Scales has authored several books about military history and strategy and continues to consult and advise in a host of venues.

TEXAS BORDER SECURITY: A STRATEGIC MILITARY ASSESSMENT

In September 2011, a nonpartisan, objective, and neutral assessment of the southern border from two of our nation's senior military officers, both with impeccable credentials, was released to the public. "Texas Border Security: A Strategic Military Assessment" covered all the angles. One of the authors (General Barry McCaffrey) had held a high-ranking post with a democratic president, and the other author (Major General Robert Scales) was an analyst with a cable news network with admittedly a few right-of-center program hosts and commentators. The report was a comprehensive, forthright and independent analysis that would give our leaders in Washington what they would need to take action and defend America.

At the beginning of the study is a graphic that should make anyone tremble with the same chilling effect from watching a George Romero horror movie like *Night of the Living Dead* or *Dawn of the Dead*. A chart with flaming red arrows shows how drug cartels are pushing violence, murder, kidnappings, torture, corruption, drugs, and many other forms of criminal behavior across the hemisphere. The arrows flow north from South and Central America into Mexico and then toward every major city in America, showing the flow of the violence perpetuated by ruthless drug cartels right into a lucrative US market.

The generals didn't mince pictures—or words:

- Crime, gangs and terrorism have converged in such a way that they form a collective threat to the national security of the United States.
- Drug cartels exploit porous borders using all the traditional elements of military force, including command and control, logistics, intelligence, information operations and the application of increasingly deadly firepower. The intention is to increasingly bring government at all levels throughout the Americas under the influence of international cartels.
- The cartels seek to gain advantage by exploiting the creases between U. S. federal and state border agencies, and the separation that exists between Mexican and American crime-fighting agencies.
- Criminality spawned in Mexico is spilling over into the United States. Texas is the tactical close combat zone and frontline in this conflict. Texans have been assaulted by cross-border gangs and narco-terrorist activities. In response, Texas has been the most aggressive and creative in confronting the threat of what has come to be a narco-terrorist military-style campaign waged against them.[65]

AN UPHILL BATTLE

You would think the report would convince the naysayers, but on October 14, 2011, the generals presented their report to a congressional subcommittee and came under a verbal assault. To add insult to injury, the attack was led by Texas Congressman Henry

Cuellar (D), Laredo, who carried the company line that the border is safer now than ever before.

Representative Cuellar presented the same FBI Uniform Crime Report data that demonstrates the crime rates in Texas border cities have gone down, but that says absolutely nothing about the rural regions where the runaround of drugs and people is occurring. These stats paint an incomplete picture and are cautioned against being used as an indicator of security by the FBI themselves! Cuellar, a capable and experienced legislator, unleashed both barrels as he challenged every aspect of the report, virtually assaulted the integrity of the generals, and claimed the border communities themselves were being attacked by this report. He boldly and flagrantly insinuated the generals were giving an inaccurate and incomplete picture, which would cause harm to the local economies.

The congressman's engagement came after I had delivered my opening remarks to the committee. I was dismayed and enraged as I sat beside the generals enduring the scolding. In a line of degrading remarks, interruptions, and bombardments on and about the report, Representative Cuellar took it to a whole other dimension when he insidiously posed, "You were paid $80,000 of taxpayer dollars to make this report, is that correct?" Now, both of these generals have been under literal fire before, and returning fire is how they earned the stars that once rested on their shoulders.

"Let me ask you, are you suggesting that this report had political or monetary motivation? If you are, sir, that is a shameful comment, and you should retract it because my dedication to this country is based on thirty-two years of service," retorted General McCaffrey in a commanding cadence that refused to be interrupted despite ongoing antagonizing from the bench where the congressman was perched. The whole exchange made for good and lively entertainment as General Scales recounted it on the Greta Van Susteren Show on FOX News a short time after the exchange occurred.

This congressman and I served together in the Texas House of Representatives and is someone I consider a friend, even though we are on different sides of the aisle and our views differ on many issues.

Henry, my friend, the border is under attack. But not by those of us seeking to protect the legal trade we enjoy. Not by those of us who support and attempt to expand the jobs from international trade. Not by those of us who promote *legal* immigration. Not by those of us who seek to protect the rights of our citizens to enjoy and use their property. As the generals said with every stroke of their pen, *violent drug cartels are trampling on America! These ruthless thugs are the enemy!*

For the sake of time at the hearing, I condensed my own verbal testimony. But the written and submitted text makes the case for what we are asking. You can read the full text in the appendix.

THERE IS NO RETREAT

"Texas Border Security: A Strategic Military Assessment" documents in unambiguous terms that we have a violently insecure, porous border with a lack of operational control. Texas is simply calling for sufficient action—ample federal resources to secure our country. No one is blaming our national leaders for the drug cartels' seedy motives and heinous actions, but saying "our border is safer than ever" signals two dangerous messages to these narco-terrorist organizations that are infiltrating America: (1) we are satisfied with the status quo, and (2) we are not going to drive you out of business. The only message from a united America should be this: *We will meet any opposing force with greater force, and we will not cede one inch of American soil!*

Texas farmers and ranchers along the US-Mexico border are regularly becoming victims of intimidation, aggression, and outright violence by armed trespassers that often have direct ties to Mexico's drug cartels. With alarming frequency, Texans along the border are subjected to physical harassment, illegal trespassing, property damage, theft, and the illegal trafficking of people and drugs on their property.

Americans should be offended that statistics are being used to diminish the crimes committed against their fellow citizens by narco-terrorists.

The reality is our porous border is a problem for all Americans—not just those at the border. Law enforcement in New York, Los Angeles, Dallas, and Houston have confirmed that cartels have gangs operating in these cities. Further, the infiltration of domestic gangs is a major component of their operational objectives.

The increases in federal support have resulted in two scenarios along the Texas-Mexico border: (1) lower major crime rates in urban border communities like

Brownsville and El Paso, and (2) a rural runaround of the drug cartels now focusing their efforts where there is the weakest presence of federal border enforcement. Keep in mind that 93 percent of the land in counties along the Texas-Mexico border is unincorporated and overwhelmingly rural.

These 2011 criminal activity summaries are a quick reminder of what these landowners endure and why we are yelling and pleading for Washington to not disregard our requests:

- February 18 – Two energy company employees were assaulted and robbed in rural Webb County
- March 11 – A ranch foreman was injured from shots fired by suspected drug cartel members in rural Webb County
- June 9 – Texas DPS and game wardens were shot at by drug traffickers in rural Hidalgo County
- June 19 – US Border Patrol was shot at by drug traffickers in an area that has seen repeated shootings aimed at US law enforcement in Hidalgo County
- July 14 – Shots were fired at water district workers in rural Hidalgo County
- September 27 – Shots were fired, killing at least one individual on Hidalgo County highway
- The personal testimony of the farmers, ranchers, and employees being told to "turn around, look the other way, and leave your property or else" while cartel members run drugs and humans through private Texas properties.

Understand that Texas is home to 64 percent of the US-Mexico border, but only 44 percent of the Border Patrol agents. There are fourteen Border Patrol agents per border mile on average from California to New Mexico. Yet there are less than half that many per mile in Texas at 6.2 agents per border mile.[66] I assure you, and so do Generals McCaffrey and Scales in their report, there is no reason for Texas to have anything but an equal or higher presence of federal law enforcement.

Targeting these terrorists and securing the border only solves part of the problem; you also must address other weaknesses that have led to the abuse of our border and laws. While I recognize these are two separate issues, it is undeniable that reducing the number of illegal entries into the United States by reforming our failed guest labor and immigration program would allow our law enforcement to focus resources on the remaining reduced illegal border crossings. Any expanded effort to secure the border would be benefited tremendously by substantially focusing on reforming a failed immigration system.

This debate can be summed up with one question: would America allow terrorists based in Canada to make nightly incursions into New York? The answer is a resounding no! We need help, and we need it now with the immediate deployment of additional boots on the ground.

Questions are still being asked, and we are still answering them. Unfortunately, some people just don't want to hear the truth.

IF YOU ARE DOING SOMETHING GOOD, THERE IS ALWAYS SOMEBODY READY TO SHOOT YOU DOWN

Having a crowd with opposite opinions on what needs to be done is not a new phenomenon to the modern age. There is never a shortage of dissenters and grumblers. Let's face it, we all have our own outlook and usually think we know best. History traces back example after example of people seeking to tear down and of one's planting dissention in order to derail the plans of another.

You think the Democrats and Republicans go after one another today? I get amused when nightly news talking heads lead this generation to believe there is something inhumane about the actions of those debating laws and policies that will guide our country. Just read David McCullough's book *John Adams* or think back to the duels between Vice President Aaron Burr and Secretary of the Treasury Alexander Hamilton, and you will get a taste of how early the struggle for position and power began in this country. But don't think it started in Colonial America. Indeed, it dates back much earlier than 1776.

Many of you have heard the Old Testament Bible story of Nehemiah, likely a native of Judah, who was living in a foreign country and serving a foreign king.

When he heard of the plight of his own people, how the wall around Jerusalem was broken down and in shambles, Nehemiah was distraught to the point of physical ailment. He asked permission of the king to return to his native country and lead in the rebuilding of the wall. Permission was granted.

Upon returning, he demonstrated leadership; he called for a better way and rallied the people. The nation found encouragement and, with great enthusiasm, began the arduous task of rebuilding from ruins.

The neighboring people took great offense to the rebuilding and took it as a sign Nehemiah was attempting to rebel against the king. Sandballot, Tobiah, and Gesham conspired time and again to disrupt the rebuilding by scheming, planting false information, and trying to discredit Nehemiah and his plans. They even conspired to wage war against those who were working on the project.

What was the response of those who were rebuilding the wall?

Nehemiah 4:17 (NIV) tells us, "Those who carried materials did their work with one hand and held a weapon in the other, and each of the builders also wore a sword at his side while he worked."

They accomplished their mission.

With pictures of dead bodies strewn along Texas ranches, with clear evidence of human trafficking, drug transports, and constant trespassing over Texas private property, why do critics continue to ridicule attempts to help our private landowners whose rights are being trampled? There are plenty of examples to demonstrate efforts to discredit the calls to defend our border and protect our people.

Dissenter 1. A story by Daniel Novick about the Protect Your Texas Border website and plight of landowners along the Texas-Mexico border was published by CW33 News in the Dallas-Ft. Worth Market on March 15, 2012. The article started out strongly conveying the unchoreographed message of multiple individuals who live and work on the border and in this region that all came to the same basic messages: it's dangerous on the border, and the politicians in Washington, DC, are not paying attention.[67]

Now Novick attempted to present a variety of perspectives on the Protect Your Texas Border website—the need, purpose, effectiveness. Among the critics he found was a professor from Southern Methodist University in Dallas.

I have been an instructor at a community college, I have been a certified instructor by state regulatory agencies and professional development institutes, and I have been a guest lecturer in classrooms across the state and world. I still have strong close ties with former professors from college and rely heavily on academic research conducted by our institutions of higher education and greatly appreciate the contributions of higher education. But if you want to get a quote that is, well, just out of touch, you can usually find someone in academia who will give that to you.

The following is an excerpt from Novick's story:

> But Rita Kirk, the director of the SMU [Southern Methodist University] Maguire

Ethics Center, said the website failed to show a strong connection between border violence and agricultural production, and she believed it was more of a political platform than a source of information.

"What we would expect from a governmental institution is to provide us facts and information that lead us to make good decisions. So we would expect there to be kind of a neutrality of facts, but factual information presented," said Kirk.

One of her biggest concerns was the "About" section of the website.

"He says, 'Texas is prepared to take matters into its own hands to the fullest extent possible.' Another phrase, 'We are at war.' So those are calls to arms," Kirk told CW 33 News.[68]

Response. Well, Director Kirk, I regret it concerns you and others that "Texas is prepared to take matters into its own hands" by deploying highly trained and qualified professional law enforcement personnel to defend our citizens, but that is just what we are doing. In fact, it would concern me greatly if Texas was not prepared to step forward in time of need.

I do not regret a Texas Ranger was quoted as saying "We are at war."[69] If you are being shot at and law enforcement officers and private citizens are being injured or killed, if you are engaged in pursuits with heavily armed criminals, if your attackers are basing their operations in a foreign country and have refuge and sanctuary being provided by some of their own law enforcement and elected officials, if many of the people threatening you are former military and use military command and control structures—then you might very well call it a war too.

I, for one, am not going to belittle the words and sacrifices being made by those who wear the uniform and carry a badge and gun protecting our country, our lives, and our way of life. I believe Americans from all over should stand beside them, and I believe they will.

And yes, there is a clear tie between agriculture production and border security and Protect Your Texas Border (I'll address the comments about politics later).

Violence is so bad on the Mexican side of the border the US Department of Agriculture stopped sending our veterinarians into Mexico to certify cattle are disease-free before being shipped into our state. Cattle are now being shipped *into our country without inspection*. USDA inspections of these animals occur at a secure holding pen inside Texas territory, and we hope this is adequately insulating us from potential disease outbreaks.

Slogans like "Where's the beef?" and "Beef, it's what's for dinner" wouldn't have found their way in the national jargon if a safe and abundant food supply wasn't serious business to Americans. In Texas, the beef cattle industry is the largest agriculture sector, and the Lone Star State is home to the nation's largest cattle herd. We have an ongoing crisis in the USA because of the heavy death toll in Mexico that is hampering best agricultural practices and resulting in enormous costs and losses to US agriculture producers. A few of these pests and diseases include the cattle fever tick, cotton boll weevil, the Asian citrus pysillid, and Mexican fruit fly that impact our $56 million citrus industry (this is cash receipts, so the economic impact of the citrus industry is much larger). Just on the Texas-Mexico border, we have 8,200 farms and ranches covering more than 15 million acres. During 2010, agricultural imports through Texas border cities totaled $8 billion, and agricultural exports through those same ports were valued at $11 billion.[70] So, yes ma'am, I'd say there is more than a clear tie between agricultural production and border security.

Ironically, this extreme and pervasive violence is having a positive economic impact in parts of the border area as people who can are fleeing the unrest and investing in American real estate. People from practically all social and economic classes are fleeing from Mexico into Texas and other states across our nation to escape the threats. As the violence has intensified over the years, the US residential real estate market has been a beneficiary, particularly in the Rio Grande Valley. One TDA employee even shared with me a story about a Mexican family that moved into an Austin apartment complex for the purpose of escaping the violence in their native country.

But clearly, border violence is taking a toll on farmers in both Texas and Mexico. Agriculture experts believe that if the violence persists, agricultural investment could shift away from Mexico, and American consumers might notice a change in where some of their food and fiber is grown.

According to C. Parr Rosson, an economist at Texas A&M University, Mexican exporters will face higher costs in the short term because tighter security at the border means longer wait times, a killer for perishable goods. Additionally, he projects that if the violence persists, Mexico's agricultural production will shift to more peaceful areas farther from the border or in the United States.[71]

Mani Skaria, a professor at Texas A&M University-Kingsville Citrus Center in Weslaco, believes long-term violence could cause farmers to consider moving operations to the United States. Some of those businesses were once in south Texas but moved to Mexico for cost savings.

"There was a time when a lot of people left the [Rio Grande] Valley to the south for cheap labor," Skaria said. "Now you might have a reversal."[72]

Some may think a reversal would be good, and we certainly welcome and encourage greater domestic food production, but the agricultural economy can be fickle. What is good for some may not be good for others. First, much of the agricultural sector is witnessing a labor shortage, so a move would only compound that problem and our immigration challenges. Secondly, American labor is generally more costly. An increase in labor costs means an increase in the prices our families will pay in the grocery stores, giving way to cheaper alternatives found abroad. The short answer here is that while we may gain in the short run, shifts and greater reliance on countries farther away brings a whole other dimension of pests, diseases, delivery challenges, and environmental and safety concerns that only complicate the reliability of our food and fiber system.

Dissenter 2. Manny Fernandez captured the sentiments of the opposition to our efforts to tell the story of the advances of the Mexican drug cartels in Texas and throughout America in a February 16, 2012, *New York Times* article.

> But the federal authorities and other local officials maintain that violent crime rates in border communities have remained flat or have decreased and that the assertions on ProtectYourTexasBorder.com are largely anecdotal. They point to other data that shows that border apprehensions in Texas have dropped 58.2 percent since 2006, and deaths along the border recorded by federal agents have decreased 6.6 percent since 2006.

Response. Those who claim the border is safer than ever hang their hat on the Federal Bureau of Investigation's Uniform Crime Report (FBI UCR). Let's take a look at what is fully being said in the UCR data and other studies published by our federal government.

GAO DATA

Here's what the US Government Accountability Office (GAO) has been saying about the southern border. Throughout its history, the GAO has operated as a nonpartisan watchdog that helps Congress monitor federal agencies and ensure accountability to taxpayers.

In February 2011, GAO testified before the United States House of Representatives, Subcommittee on Border and Maritime Security, at a hearing titled "Securing Our Borders: Operational Control and the Path Forward."

While the whole document titled "Border Security: Preliminary Observations on Border Control Measures for the Southwest Border" prepared by the GAO is certainly worth reading, just glancing through the first few pages clearly demonstrates the statistics support the conclusion of a monumental problem. It vividly proves the point and backs up the "personal observations" of the landowners who are being terrorized!

The opening statement by Richard M. Stana, director of Homeland Security and Justice Issues, GAO, is best conveyed in his own words:

> "Chairwoman Miller, Ranking Member Cuellar, and Members of the Subcommittee:
>
> I am pleased to be here today to discuss issues regarding the Department of Homeland Security's (DHS) process for measuring security for the nearly 2,000-mile U.S. border with Mexico. *DHS reports that the southwest border continues to be vulnerable to cross-border illegal activity, including the smuggling of humans and illegal narcotics.* The Office of Border Patrol (Border Patrol), within DHS's U.S. Customs and Border Protection (CBP), is the federal agency with primary responsibility for securing the border between the U.S. ports of entry. CBP has divided geographic responsibility for southwest border miles among nine Border

Patrol sectors, as shown in figure 1. CBP reported spending about $3 billion to support Border Patrol's efforts on the southwest border in fiscal year 2010, and *Border Patrol reported apprehending over 445,000 illegal entries and seizing over 2.4 million pounds of marijuana.*[73] (Emphasis added. Also remember, elsewhere BP estimates 75 percent evades apprehension!)

This is just the beginning of the GAO repeating Homeland Security's own information and conveying it in a manner that undoubtedly describes the gaping holes in our border.

Another pertinent excerpt from the report is the quote that demonstrates how porous our border actually is. It is a fact that the statistics don't always paint the complete picture, and anecdotal evidence is important. Some have attacked our efforts on ProtectYourTexasBorder.com because the site includes interviews with farmers and ranchers who have bravely come forward to relay their experience with the violence along the border. Some critics dismiss these firsthand accounts as anecdotal, not scientific. However, the GAO testimony demonstrates the importance of anecdotal evidence:

"Border Patrol reported achieving varying levels of operational control of 873 (44 percent) of the nearly 2,000 southwest border miles at the end of fiscal year 2010. The number of reported miles under operational control increased an average of 126 miles per year from fiscal years 2005 through 2010 (see fig. 2). Border Patrol sector officials

assessed the miles under operational control using factors such as operational statistics, third-party indicators, intelligence and operational reports, resource deployments, and discussions with senior Border Patrol agents.[6] Border Patrol officials attributed the increase in operational control to deployment of additional infrastructure, technology, and personnel along the border.[7] For example, from fiscal years 2005 through 2010, the number of border miles that had fences increased from about 120 to 649 and the number of Border Patrol agents increased from nearly 10,000 to more than 17,500 along the southwest border."[74]

The footnote references for this section read:

[6]Operational statistics generally include the number of apprehensions and known illegal border entries and volume and shift of smuggling activity, among other performance indicators. Border Patrol officials at sectors and headquarters convene to discuss and determine the number of border miles under operational control for each sector based on relative risk.[75]

The translation: statistics may be skewed because much illegal activity goes unreported, and it is important to hear from the boots on the ground when making a comprehensive assessment. I sure wish Secretary Napolitano and President Obama would realize that they should be listening to those *cowboy* boots on the ground.

Well, 44 percent up from 0 percent is good. But what does this mean for the 56 percent of the remainder of the border that does not fall within "varying levels of operational control"? If you are a landowner who lives, works, and raises your family along stretches of the Rio Grande, would you want to be among the 44 percent that is considered being under operational control or the 56 percent that is outside of this area?

Particularly telling is language in this next paragraph, language about prioritizing:

> Across the southwest border, Yuma sector reported achieving operational control for all of its border miles. In contrast, the other southwest border sectors reported achieving *operational control ranging from 11 to 86 percent of their border miles* [see fig. 3]. Border Patrol officials attributed the *uneven progress across sectors* to multiple factors, including terrain, transportation infrastructure on both sides of the border, and *a need to prioritize resource deployment to sectors deemed to have greater risk of illegal activity.*[76]

The above is what the landowners in the rural regions are asking for! In the government's own language, please "prioritize resource deployment to sectors deemed to have greater risk of illegal activity."

If a picture is worth a thousand words, this bar chart is worth ten thousand!

SOUTHWEST BORDER MILES UNDER OPERATIONAL CONTROL BY BORDER PATROL SECTOR, AS OF SEPTEMBER 30, 2010

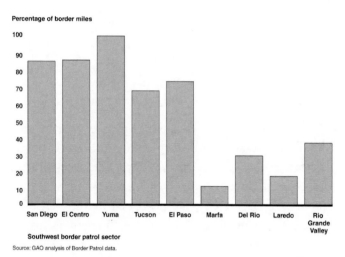

Percentage of border miles

Southwest border patrol sector

Source: GAO analysis of Border Patrol data.

Border Patrol reported that the sectors had made progress toward gaining control of some of the 1,120 southwest border miles that were not yet under operational control. Border Patrol reported an increased ability to detect, respond, or interdict illegal activity for more than 10 percent of these southwest border miles from fiscal year 2009 to September 30, 2010.

San Diego to Yuma tells one story, Tucson to El Paso another, and Marfa to Rio Grande Valley yet another. Looking at this data and the wide disparity in operational control by sector unmistakably reveals not all portions of the border are equal in terms of "operational control." This reminds me of the old story about the definition of recession and depression. If your neighbor is out of work, it is a recession. If you are out of work, it is a depression. People who live along the areas where there is such a lack of operational control of the southern US border have a compelling reason to be depressed. They don't have to be depressed from their own observations (which our government says cannot be trusted); they can just look at this government-generated bar chart and pine away.

FBI UCR DATA

Doubters claim the situation of border security is *better than ever* and continually dismiss urgent pleas for more assistance because of the rankings and reporting of the Federal Bureau of Investigation's Uniform Crime Reports (UCR). UCRs are described by the FBI as "a voluntary city, university and college, county, state, tribal, and federal law enforcement program that provides a nationwide view of crime based on the submission of statistics by law enforcement agencies throughout the country."[77]

Eight major crime categories are included in the UCR and are as follows:

1. Murder and non-negligent manslaughter
2. Forcible rape
3. Robbery
4. Aggravated assault
5. Burglary
6. Larceny theft
7. Motor vehicle theft
8. Arson

These crimes are plenty dreadful, no doubt. But what if you were, say, kidnapped? Wouldn't you want that included? How about bribery and public corruption? Do you think plain assault as compared to aggravated assault is something to be considered?

Kidnapping, bribery, extortion, money laundering, drug dealing, human trafficking, indentured servitude, and public corruption is the very activity of the drug cartels, and yet these are not included in the UCR! We also have testimony from witnesses who refused to go on record for fear of retaliation, which leads you to the unanswered question of "Just how many of these type of crimes are not being reported?"

Is intimidation and being told to leave your own land a serious offense in your opinion? Constant trespassing to the point that well-worn trails have beaten down the grass and brush is a major issue if you are the landowner. What if your fences were cut and pushed down repeatedly and gates left open where your source of making a living (livestock) is turned loose, and you were in continuous roundup and repair mode on your own property?

What if you couldn't sell your property because of the constant crime? What if you could no longer earn much-needed income by leasing your land for hunting because of the violence that occurs but is not captured in the FBI UCR? Regrettably, market participants are not relying on the same set of "data" as those that claim our border is safer than ever.

I think the FBI is a crucially important component to fighting crime in America. I am thankful for the agents and intelligence operations that work around the clock while millions of Americans sleep restfully. But to those that wave the UCR and say there is no problem, I say read all of the FBI's disclaimers that are published right alongside and sometimes in front of the UCR data:

> *Disclaimers.* Since crime is a sociological phenomenon influenced by a variety of factors, the FBI discourages ranking the agencies and using the data as a measurement of law enforcement effectiveness (www.fbi.gov/about-us/cjis/ucr/word).
>
> Each year when crime in the United States is published, many entities—news media, tourism agencies, and other groups with an interest in crime in our nation—use reported figures to compile rankings of cities and counties. These rankings, however, are merely a quick choice made by the data user; they provide no insight into the many variables that mold the crime in a particular town, city, county, state, region, or other jurisdiction. *Consequently, these rankings lead to simplistic and/or incomplete analyses that often create misleading perceptions adversely affecting cities and counties along with their residents.*
>
> Crime in the United States provides a nationwide view of crime based on statistics contributed by local, state, tribal, and federal law enforcement agencies. Population size and student enrollment are the only correlates of crime presented in this publication. Although many of the listed factors equally affect the

crime of a particular area, the UCR program makes no attempt to relate them to the data presented. *The data user is, therefore, cautioned against comparing statistical data of individual reporting units from cities, counties, metropolitan areas, states, or colleges or universities solely on the basis of their population coverage or student enrollment. Until data users examine all the variables that affect crime in a town, city, county, state, region, or other jurisdiction, they can make no meaningful comparisons.*[78]

If you want to talk statistics, answer this simple question. If the border is so safe, how are drugs, weighed by the ton, being shipped north, and cash, counted in the billions, flowing south? By our own federal government reports, a minimum of $9 billion and upward of $22 billion is flowing south in exchange for illegal substances in America.[79] If our border is so safe and no more help is needed, how are these drugs arriving in every major city in America? Well, the tooth fairy isn't bringing them.

The late Arizona Cochise County Sherrif Larry Dever put it in perspective in his interview with NBC.

> In Cochise County, Ariz., which shares an 84-mile-long border with Mexico, Sheriff Larry Dever was among many border officials who did not laugh at President Obama's joke about moats and alligators. "I can't tell you how angry it made not only me, but my constituents, to make a mockery of one of the most serious situations we face in our entire lifetime," he

said. "I'd say the border is more dangerous than it's ever been."

Dever has lost four friends—three police officers and a rancher—to cartel violence, and insists Mexican traffickers crossing into his county are well-armed and much more aggressive now than they were just a few years ago. "We're getting overrun from the south, because the federal government isn't doing its job," he said.

The long-time sheriff argued that the FBI Uniform Crime Report statistics cited by the White House fail to include many of the crimes committed by traffickers, including kidnapping, extortion, public corruption, drug and human smuggling, and trespassing. "I invite them to come down here, come live with us and go camp out at some rancher's house and see what happens at night," he said. When asked if anyone from Washington had ever agreed to do that, Dever said, "Heck no, they come for photo ops."[80]

TEXAS EVIDENCE

Police and law enforcement reports can be good tools, when used appropriately and in conjunction with other appropriate data. The Texas Department of Public Safety has modernized and evolved in order to provide a higher level of security and crime-fighting strength that Texans demand. The DPS website has chronicled serious activity in America, not Mexico, which confirms the active efforts of the cartels to ensure their trade continues.

Major multi-agency investigations have resulted in the arrest of hundreds of Mexican cartel members and associates who operated in Texas. Since 2007, these arrests have included at least 81 from the Gulf Cartel, 9 from the Juarez Cartel, 149 from La Familia Michoacana, 66 from Los Zetas, and 2 from the Sinaloa Cartel.[81]

Since 2009, there have been twenty-five documented homicides in Texas related to cartel criminal activity. The assessment of whether a crime was related to the Mexican cartels is based upon the best available information from ongoing investigations, confidential informants, and intelligence reporting. Crimes linked to the cartels will be added or, in some instances, reduced based upon new information to indicate that it was or was not related to the Mexican cartels.[82]

SHERIFF'S FIRSTHAND OBSERVATIONS

Sheriff Clint McDonald of Terrell County, Texas, has not been bashful about conveying the urgency of the need for help fighting the Mexican drug cartel members on the Texas side of the border. It has been roughly calculated that Sheriff McDonald has one deputy for less than every four hundred square miles.

His story is summarized in "A Field Investigation Report of the House Immigration Reform Caucus" by Immigration Reform Caucus Chairman Brian Bilbray and House Republican Conference Secretary John Carter:

Sheriff Clint McDonald's department has a total of 7 officers, with one on the road at a given time to patrol 54 miles of river border with 22 crossings. Terrell County's population of only 1200 prohibits any expansion of law enforcement activities without state or federal assistance.

Sheriff McDonald says the majority of his activities are in response to illegal alien activity, with illegal aliens committing as high as 90% of burglaries in the county in what has become a pattern of cross border raids by Mexican burglars.

McDonald says that until the Mexican drug wars erupted along with the U.S. recession, the majority of illegal alien activity in the county was by economic migrants. The majority of activity now consists of criminal activity and drug smuggling.

Sheriff McDonald reports a good working relationship with the Border Patrol, and that the recent Operation Easter Demonstration Project in the Big Bend area was a total success. The Sheriff reaffirmed that there is and can be no cross border communications or cooperation with Mexican law enforcement due to the total corruption from the drug wars.

Sheriff McDonald testifies that his river border is so rugged, with massive canyon walls over the river that the only places that illegals can realistically cross on his 54 mile border are at the 22 specific crossings mentioned earlier. Therefore National Guard teams posted at those crossings would virtually cease illegal entries into Terrell County, with an estimated 200 troops necessary for the job. McDonald says there are potential issues with such a deployment that must be addressed to succeed, however. The troops must be armed and on the river, not a mile or miles back as is the current Border Patrol.

Property owners also have reluctance to allow the National Guard on their property under the terms offered by the Department of Homeland Security during Operation Jumpstart.

Unlike the Border Patrol which has legal authority to enter private property within 25 miles of the U.S. border, the National Guard has no such right, and entry must be voluntarily granted by the landowner. Many landowners were initially willing to verbally allow entry under condition their roads, fences, and livestock not be damaged, similar to the entry permission most grant to their Sheriff. However, DHS drew up detailed legal waivers for landowners to sign with liability clauses and acknowledgements of extensive military operations on their land that landowners rejected as overreaching and unnecessary.

Any future deployments in which National Guardsmen needed to access private land would be more successfully conducted by having the Guard co-ordinate with landowners exclusively through the local Sheriff rather than DHS or other federal authorities. Most other Texas Sheriffs interviewed during the field investigation agreed with Sheriff McDonalds' evaluation.[83]

Dissenter 3: Focusing on the differences. NBC Nightly News published a March 15, 2012, story titled "Debate Rages Over Mexico 'Spillover Violence' in US." The lead-off teaser for the story was this: "In the middle of a presidential election year, there's a big debate between Democrats and Republicans, and law enforcement and ranchers, over how much violence from the Mexican drug war has spilled over into the United States, making it hard to get straight answers."[84]

Response. I agree there is a difference between many Democrats and Republicans on this breach of national security, but local media are calling the violence out for what it is, and so do many of the local law enforcement officials.

Several of the Texas border counties' chief-elected law enforcement officials have banded together to form the Texas Border Sheriff's Coalition, a nonprofit organization headquartered in El Paso. Most, if not all, of their members are Democratic elected officials in the county of which they are sheriff. One particular sheriff, Sigifredo "Sigi" Gonzalez Jr. (D) is seldom shy about telling it like it is, is not particularly fond of any political administration, and says this is far from a Democratic or Republican matter but rather one of safety and security.

In a YouTube posting, Sheriff Gonzalez comes out blazing in the opening lines: "Our US border is still controlled really by the Mexican drug trafficking organizations because they control the Mexican border who comes across and what comes across obviously they will also control this side of the border also."

The sheriff is a Democrat, and his story is consistent with democratically elected Sheriff Clint McDonald of Terrell County, whose story has been recounted elsewhere in this book. Neither of these gentlemen is trying to make this a partisan political issue. To them it is a life-and-death issue, a survival issue; it is not about propaganda, but it is about protection.

I encourage you to listen to the entire interview by Sheriff Gonzalez where he also says it is totally different than it used to be and discusses automatic weapons being used. The interview can be found on youtube.com by searching Sheriff Gonzales.

YOU WIN SOME, YOU LOSE SOME, BUT ALWAYS FINISH THE GAME

The issue of border security should not be a partisan issue. We are talking about people's safety and livelihoods. We know there will be differences wider than the Grand Canyon when it comes to tax policy or wealth redistribution or Obamacare, and only the people exercising their constitutional right to vote will determine the direction of these controversial issues. The media certainly plants bait to entice lively debate on these issues to fill the evening news.

I have participated in my share of fighting for what I believe to be the right course for Texas and America. I'm not one to play the victim card, but I can tell you that after numerous campaigns and twenty years in some form of elected service, it sure seems like conservatives take the most punches from the media. But on the border security issue, many in the media are working hard to call balls and strikes.

KRGV is a television station located in the Rio Grande Valley and based in Weslaco, Texas. They spend a great deal of time and resources in reporting the events in their viewing area. They have some great stories to tell about the success and economic expansion of this vibrant region of our country. Reporters like Jordan Williams, Farrah Fazal, Erica Proffer and Joe Augustine do not shy away from reporting on the atrocities associated with cartel violence. I urge you to go to their website, www.krgv.com, and type the word *cartel* in their search engine on their home page. The day I did it, I got 644 hits or matches.

KURV is a radio station with studios in McAllen, Texas, and bills itself as "the Valley's News, Weather, and Talk Station." They have very active drive-time call-in talk and news formats anchored by Sergio Sanchez and Tim Sullivan and cover Valley, state, and national news quite extensively. They constantly cover spillover border crime.

I assume the doubters would call the news stories these two outlets publish propaganda, too, but you must remember these media outlets are in the middle of the activity they report on. To those who are the victims in these stories, they call them real life.

There are many examples to pull from when it comes to what is being reported along our southwest border with Mexico. Out of all the national news media, FOX News has probably covered the spillover violence and infiltration by the transnational terrorists more than any other. They ran a segment called "America's Third War." Major show anchor Greta Van Susteren has been to our southwestern border with Mexico many times and has seen the activities firsthand. From Bill O'Reilly, Sean Hannity, and Megyn Kelly in studio to Chris Guttierez on the ground, story after story has documented facts and firsthand testimony of the atrocities.

SOLUTIONS REQUIRE WORK AND LEADERSHIP

My father was not the kind to go around quoting scripture, although he read them frequently. I do distinctly remember him consistently quoting these verses found in Proverbs:

> A little sleep, A little slumber,
> a little folding of the hands to rest—
> and poverty will come on you like a bandit
> and scarcity like an armed man.
>
> Proverbs 6:10-11 (NIV)

If our country is not focused on a solution and does not demonstrate the resolve to work at all costs to win this battle, when will our landowners get relief and our nation's security be ensured? This is no time to quote misplaced statistics and obscure data that has no relevance to the reality of the fresh footprints that are found on a daily basis.

We need committed leadership. Leadership is about wisely developing a vision, energizing and coalescing others around the goal, and carrying through.

Here's my vision on border security: I do not support, condone, or encourage vigilante justice. I do support someone defending themselves, their family, and their property. I support the right to keep and bear arms that is guaranteed in the Second Amendment of the Bill of Rights. I do support treating "our neighbors as ourselves" and "doing unto others as we would have them do unto us." I also expect others to abide by this philosophy if they desire it to be extended to them.

Providing an environment where jobs can flourish and all can enjoy our free market enterprise system is my goal, and I refuse to leave one segment of our economy behind. Jobs will not take a backseat to border security, and a secure border and available jobs are both essential to our future prosperity.

I do support and defend the rights of states to exercise the powers reserved to them under the United States Constitution, and particularly those rights not enumerated to the federal government. I also expect the federal government to fully exercise its role, responsibility, and obligation in defending and protecting our domestic security interests from foreign incursions. When the headquarters of these criminal organizations are based outside of our country and yet plan, plot, and connive ways to subvert our laws and purvey their product and pain on our soil, we cannot say "Mission accomplished" until those who are bearing the brunt are prepared to say thank you for restoring our dignity. The day for "thank you" has not yet arrived.

TO KNOW WHERE YOU'RE GOING, YOU NEED TO LOOK WHERE YOU'VE BEEN

Why did people develop and form the Colonies? Why did waves of Europeans come to the New World and settle an untamed country? Mankind has a curiosity that transcends generations and cultural divides, and history continues to confirm that necessity is the mother of invention.

We were taught the Pilgrims immigrated to escape religious persecution...or even legal prosecution. Historians offer us a wide view of the pathway that led to the shores of the New World. The view of a Frenchman, only a visitor to our developing country during the nineteenth century, gives us a glimpse of who came to America.

Alexis de Tocqueville provides us with the words of those who came in 1620 themselves: "For the glory of God, and advancement of the Christian faith, and the honor of our king and country a voyage to plant the first colony in the northern parts of Virginia."[85]

Persecuted by the authorities of Europe, Tocqueville explicitly relays the motivations of the migration of some from the Old World to the New by reporting, "The Puritans sought a land so barbarous and neglected by the world that there at last they might be able to live in their own way and pray to God in freedom."[86]

Lest we become too pious in our view of our forbearers, he also included motives not so celestial in their origins.

> It was therefore gold-seekers who were sent to Virginia, men without wealth or standards whose restless, turbulent temper endangered the infant colony and made its progress vacillating. Craftsman and farm laborers came later; they were quieter folk with better morals, but there was hardly any respect in which they rose above the level of the English lower classes.[87]

An aristocracy was surely left across the ocean. To further ensure we have the right perspective about who we are as a nation and where all we came from, Tocqueville continued with words to enlighten and to keep forever humble modern-day America.

> In almost all other colonies the first inhabitants have been men without wealth or education, driven from their native land by poverty or misconduct, or else greedy speculators and industrial entrepreneurs.[88]

From the well-to-do to the ne'er-do-well, the origins of America are colorful and storied. Few can rightly make a noble claim, and few can rightly claim the end result is not noble.

Looking back always provides a clearer vision than looking forward, but with such a variety of early Americans, it is sometimes hard to conceive the pages of our past are so wrought with the "pulling up the ladder" syndrome. This phenomena of "once you get in the boat (become licensed to do business), make it harder for the next wave to join you" is something that seems instinctively a part of all mankind, and the pages of American history prove we are cut from the same cloth of greed, envy, and fear that each generation must overcome if we are to maintain lasting success and prosperity.

Waves of Irish and German Catholics gave rise to an "antiforeign feeling" in the 1840s and 1850s and, in part, is said to be attributed to those of English Protestant ancestry having a "fear" of the Roman Catholic church. Because some immigrants to America during the pre-Civil War period had been engaged in European revolutions, the perception arose that immigrants are associated with revolutionary activity and attacks on government.

If resentment was bad toward immigrants in the decades beginning in the 1840s, it is said "the 1880s and 1890s provoked even greater fear and hostility." The influx of population in response to the poor world conditions and the rising industrialization of America led to the belief by many already established in this country that the high rate of birth among this wave of immigrants would rapidly leave the established Americans to "soon be outbred and outvoted."[89]

Below are other relevant thoughts said to be prevalent during the course of the last one hundred years of immigration and growth toward those who landed on US soil:

- "Fear of foreign radicalism and subversion was another powerful force in creating prejudice."
- "Native-born workers often greeted the new immigrants with hostility."
- A labor movement that was directed toward the Chinese is stated to have developed into a "hate campaign" that led to the passage of legislation in 1882 called the Chinese Exclusion Act, which had the effect of "cutting off all Chinese immigration for ten years."
- "In 1917, Congress passed a law, over President Wilson's veto, denying admittance to aliens over age sixteen who were unable to read in any language."
- "By 1920 the Japanese were legally prohibited from leasing or buying land in California."[90]

Recognizing and remembering these incidences are a part of our nation's past can guide us to the future where our country avoids the pitfalls that ensnared earlier generations.

Accusations of racism fill the stories of our nation's newspapers as the country deals with a violently porous border today that doesn't discriminate among those seeking a job (this too is breaking the law when coming into the country without proper documentation) and those seeking to do us harm.

Some people are racists—plain and simple. It is sad, and it includes whites harboring prejudice against people of other color such as blacks or Latinos, blacks who clutch ill will toward Asians and Latinos who have these same feelings toward people of other skin color. People of some faith or belief also engage in discrimination. The list could go on and on here, but we cannot and must not allow those with unjust motives to guide our national debate.

Shortly after launching the Protect Your Texas Border website, in a letter sent to me authored by State Senator Rodriguez, he implores me to remove the website immediately, saying it "does nothing more than create a forum that has already been used to promote violence and hate."

In a blog published by the *Houston Chronicle*, I was publically challenged by US Congressman Reyes who said of the report authored and published by two of our nation's top and highly decorated generals, one of whom was the drug czar under President Clinton:

> These claims are only distracting Texans from the real issues facing our state. Indeed, this is all smoke and mirrors...they focus on bills that suppress minority and elderly voter turnout, and others that tie the hands of local law enforcement agencies reaching out to Latino communities, all to promote...political agenda.[91]

Sadly, neither of these two elected officials (I have since met with them both) offered any comment in these articles about the need to protect our citizens who are being trampled on by these out-of-control criminal organizations. They tried to inject race into this tragic situation that negatively impacts both

Latinos and Anglos indiscriminately. In fact, the crime being perpetrated against citizens of our United States is an area that I can attest knows no boundaries and is prejudice-free. Shameless drug dealers have proven over and over they will terrorize anyone of any color or gender or age who stands in their way. The website being criticized has testimony from both Anglo and Latino Americans who passionately describe their firsthand accounts of terror.

As we move forward with defending our borders and reforming our failed immigration system, we must do so in terms of being *pro*–legal immigration to distinguish from the race-baiting that plagued our country in the past and remains a part of the dialogue today. To do otherwise is to dishonor the price paid to move this country forward and ignores the pain and suffering endured by so many for so long.

Americans can do better. Americans will do better.

A FRAMEWORK FOR REFORM

Having worked on legislation for a number of years, I know big, complex, thorny problems usually take a while to get it right…and then only time will tell if it is right or not.

Political opponents rapidly seize upon opportunities to point out flaws in introduced legislation that will bear no semblance to the final document that will undergo public hearing, expert testimony, and committee and floor debates—a process that is duplicated in each legislative chamber.

Even after the thorough process, there are still some who seek out the perfect over the good. Personally, I've never seen any perfect legislation. That is why government doing as little as possible is usually the best position for the people in the big picture of things. I'll never forget the conversation I had on the floor of the Texas House of Representatives my freshman year. A senior member came up after the deadline had passed for filing legislation for the session and asked how many bills I had filed.

I replied, "None."

He laughed condescendingly and said, "I filed over eighty bills!"

I remember nervously shaking my head as I walked away because my constituents thought we have too many laws, not too few. I didn't seek office to file bills as much as I did to stop bad things from happening from a government that could be too big and could spend too much money. I sought office to limit government's efforts to do too many things for too many people, all with other people's money, which leads to a seemingly inescapable cycle of dependency. But I digress.

So there are some things government should do.

As we have fought for resources to secure our southern border, as we have pled for greater assistance and enhanced measures to protect our landowners from being chased off their own lands, it has become painfully obvious we must reduce the flow of traffic with which they must contend. Let's be smart about our enforcement and eliminate the volume of traffic that can be minimized by reforming our failed immigration system. No one can deny that it would be much easier to sort through ten people per night trying to illegally enter our country than it would be to stop one hundred. Can you imagine the enhanced effectiveness of our existing law enforcement if our eight thousand Texas-based Border Patrol were focusing on and solely targeting drug runners? What an impact this would have on reducing the violence that has spilled over onto American soil. Reducing the numbers entering our country illegally is undoubtedly a major component to leveraging the resources we have and to enabling our dedicated law enforcement to do their job.

EVERYBODY'S GOT A PLAN

We know there are dozens upon dozens of concepts and strategies for securing our border and resolving our immigration dilemma. Opinions are like, well, let's say…noses. Everybody's got one.

History has shown that developing a pathway forward shouldn't include a pathway to citizenship, or at least it shouldn't if we want to help fix the impasse rather than perpetuate one.

Developing a framework to deal with the issues that divide us is a major step toward solving the predicament. While there are many factors and countless suggested solutions, the acronym SEDMRP (defined soon) outlines the key elements necessary to solving the big problems and avoids kicking the can down the road. Solving part of the problem only makes things worse as the clever resourcefulness of man tends to surpass the good intentions of mankind.

So it is vital to understand these issues are meant to be implemented together, simultaneously, in conjunction with one another. Just as when the 1986 reforms were passed, only a portion of the compact was completed and the efforts failed to meet the objectives of America, so too will efforts in 2013 or beyond if we fail to think broadly and implement cohesively. Many have commented on the failures of the Immigration and Control Act of 1986, but a major recurring theme, as pointed out by President Reagan's own attorney general at the time, is that employer sanctions were not strictly enforced.[92]

I would add that the reason it was not enforced, and one of the reasons illegal immigration persists today, is because of market demands. An adequate labor force, guest or domestic, through legal means was not provided.

Republicans pride ourselves on being defenders of the free market (as we should). An important precept to heed is that if government actions fail to address a matter, the market usually can and does adjust to compensate (and do so much more effectively).

It is also important to point out what then US Senate candidate Marco Rubio articulated in a November 2009 Post on Politics article by George Bennett. Rubio said of the results of the 1986 act:

> It was easier to do the amnesty program than it was to do the legal process. In other words, people seeking access to America rightly surmised, "Why come to the United States of America through legal immigration when the government of the United States made illegal entry through amnesty a more preferable process?"[93]

Rubio's comments obviously resonated with a majority of Florida voters as he handily won the US Senate seat in 2010, although he did it without a majority thanks to former Republican Florida governor Charlie Crist's independent candidacy.

Rubio's sentiment is a reflection of what most people intuitively know—people tend to take the path of least resistance. And the ingenuity of people will develop alternative paths to artificial or weak barriers.

THOSE WHO FAIL TO PLAN, PLAN TO FAIL

Here we go. SEDMRP — a framework for reform.

> **S**ecure our border
> **E**nforce our laws
> **D**ocument all immigrants
> **M**andate country-of-origin application for citizenship
> **R**eform failed visa system
> **P**orts must be modernized

S: SECURE OUR BORDER

It is first because it is essential to sending the right message. Securing our border must be the first step because if we concede we have a tolerance for those who openly break our laws and flout their disregard for our governing system, no matter the intentions, we fail. And, friend, failure is not an option.

A secure border is critical for defending our nation against terrorism and transnational criminal organizations (TCOs) that traffic illegal drugs, weapons, and people. The federal government has failed to meet the evolving and constant threat posed by TCOs. No immigration system can function without a secure border.

Specific steps are needed to secure our southern border. Tangible actions are needed to support the valiant efforts of our local sheriff departments, city police, state law enforcement, and border patrol between the ports of entry and augment the billions of dollars our federal government spends annually to secure our border. These actions include the following:

- Categorize cartel violence as a global terroristic threat[94] that threatens our allies and citizens. Cripple them financially by going after their funding and resources and eliminate their ability to launder their ill-gotten gains.
- Commit more resources to confront this terrorism by bringing uniformity to the number of border patrol agents per border mile. Consider re-positioning of border patrol agents. As South Texas rancher Joseph Fitzsimons reflects, *Why not stop them where they are crossing, the border? We know they are there.*
- Increase National Guard troop strength stationed at the border. Explore ways to conduct annual training of these troops in the remote areas of the border, on federal lands, and in cooperation with private landowners.
- Change tactics to allow forceful engagement and effective cross-border enforcement.
- Equip landowners with tools to secure their property, including expanding the number of security cameras, brush eradication program, land sensors, and report hotlines.
- As the wars in Iran and Afghanistan come to a close, bring home the billions of dollars of surplus military equipment that has been used to secure foreign borders and secure our own. Give border states the first priority use of the *quality* equipment such as night vision paraphernalia, surveillance cameras, advanced communication and detection devices, armored vehicles and air assets, etc.

- Consider even greater partnerships with local sheriffs and city police as their deputies and officers know the border geography, know the people, know the culture, and are directly accountable to the local citizens and landowners who are bearing the brunt of the invasions. Be prepared to adequately fund overtime.

"Sic vis pacum, pare bellum." I once read a United States Marine reference the above Latin phrase, which is an axiom Americans have understood and lived by for the last few decades. Translated, it simply but profoundly means "If you want peace, prepare for war."

No one knows for certain the 100 percent efficient and politically palpable remedy to cure our woes of a porous border that allows people into our country seeking to do us harm. But one thing we Americans do know that works, and that is the relentless, uncompromising pursuit of a goal will lead to victory.

E: ENFORCE OUR LAWS

Let me ask you a question. Okay, be honest with yourself. If you are driving down a long, straight stretch of remote highway and you are pretty confident you are alone, do you have the tendency to maybe exceed the posted speed limit a bit? I wonder what the compliance rate would be with our income tax laws if there were no audits or the threat of audits?

For laws to work, they must be enforced. Our country can no longer accept a "wink and a nod" approach to our employment laws and ever expect to solve our illegal immigration predicament. Neither should our nation expect our employers to become immigration police themselves. We need a system that does enforce our laws. Remember what Attorney General Meese said of the inept 1986 act? It was so in part due to the lack of the employer sanction enforcement.

Now, if you are an employer, keep reading. This is not the final part of the broad reform effort; it is just a portion of it. However, all citizens should have to abide by the laws of the land. If we do not like the laws, we should change them. In this case, lackadaisical enforcement has simply perpetuated the volume of people who are unauthorized to be in our country. Enforcing our laws will correct this situation and, again, is a *part* of the solution.

Some insist, "Take action now; just enforce the laws we have!" When doing so, though, keep in mind it must be contingent upon also ensuring our government reforms the failed visa system that is so cumbersome and inefficient, particularly for agriculture, construction, and hospitality.

And, don't forget, enforcing our laws is not just directed toward employment scenarios. President Obama's isolated decision to selectively enforce immigration laws on young illegal immigrants and to only deport certain classes of illegal immigrants absolutely undermines the entire immigration system. Why would anyone try to use a cumbersome and costly legal system when the president of the United States gives you an alternative route? His actions only reinforce the need to come together as a nation and solve this problem.

D: DOCUMENT ALL IMMIGRANTS

At a time when rural, remote portions of our border serve as a portal for drug cartels and criminal organizations to terrorize our landowners and distribute illegal narcotics, we also know that OTMs (law enforcement's acronym for people from countries other than Mexico who are entering the United States illegally) from countries known to support terrorism are also infiltrating America.

I went to the US Department of Homeland Security's website to find recent information about how many OTMs had crossed into our country. Using their search engine, I typed in *OTM* and hit Enter. After choosing an option to not delete any queries that looked repetitive, I received a total of five links to choose from. The descriptions talked a lot about FOIA (Freedom of Information Act), so I chose the only one I saw that mentioned OTM in the commentary under the link. It is shown below.

> FOIA Activity for the Week of December 25, 2009–January 1...
> ...OTMs) detained at the US border or at other checkpoints inside of the United States for 2007, 2008 and 2009 and whether the **OTM** were returned... www.dhs.gov/xlibrary/assets/foia/chief-foia-officer-weekly-report-2010-redacted.PDF–2011-10-03

Being somewhat adventurous and feeling the need for this information, I clicked the link, and this was the first title on the 301-page document:

> FOIA Activity for the Week of December 25, 2009–January 1, 2010
> Privacy Office
> January 4, 2009
> Weekly FOIA Report

I wish I were kidding, but I'm not. All I could see was a long list of FOIA reports, week by week, and related information. Maybe the information I sought was there, but if so, they did a good job burying it. So I typed in "other than Mexico," hoping I was just not adept at the DHS web search tools. Well, after glancing through the first two pages of suggested links with every article with the words *other*, *than*, and *Mexico* and with those words not being together, I decided to go another route. Thank goodness for Judicial Watch's website.

Judicial Watch apparently filed one of those FOIA request themselves because they issued a press release on March 9, 2011, titled "Judicial Watch Obtains New Border Patrol Apprehension Statistics for Illegal Alien Smugglers and 'Special Interest Aliens.'"[96]

Highlights from the FOIA, seemingly reflecting FY 2010 apprehensions, cited in the release are as follows:

- US Border Patrol agents apprehended 463,382 individuals smuggled across the border, including 8,905 smugglers (3,027 of the smugglers apprehended were deemed "deportable").

- US Border Patrol agents apprehended 59,017 "other than Mexican" illegal aliens through October 7, 2010.
- Among the nations represented in apprehension statistics are the four countries currently on the state department's list of "State Sponsors of Terrorism": Cuba (712), Iran (14), Syria (5) and Sudan (5), as well as Somalia (9), Afghanistan (9), Pakistan (37), Saudi Arabia (5), and Yemen (11).
- Overall, US Border Patrol agents apprehended 663 "aliens from special interest countries." These countries are deemed special interest because of their suspected ties to terrorism.
- The countries yielding the highest "other than Mexican" apprehensions include Guatemala (18,406), El Salvador (13,723), and Honduras (13,580).[97]

These aliens from special interest countries should be alarming enough to make everyone realize, especially policymakers responsible for protecting and securing the United States's people, that it is false to claim that "the border is better than ever." Come on, Secretary Napolitano, who are you kidding? The numbers in this report are your numbers—straight from the United States Department of Homeland Security.

Why do I not feel secure?

The release also stated "US Border Patrol estimates that three out of every four illegal aliens who cross the border evade apprehension."

Okay, quiz time.

Question: if the border patrol estimates 75 percent of the illegal aliens who cross the border evade apprehension and they apprehended 463,382 individuals in FY 2010, how many illegal aliens crossed the border in fiscal year 2010?

Answer:1,853,528 illegal aliens crossed into the United States of America in FY 2010.

Let's do fifth grade math verification (okay, maybe sixth or eighth grade; long time ago here, but now I am actually glad they made me do this in school):

1,853,528 illegal aliens
× 25% apprehended (75% don't get caught, so that
leaves 25% who do, right?)
463,382   Correct!

Does this really mean *almost two million* illegal aliens crossed into the United States of America in 2010? Safer than ever or alarming? I wish President Obama would answer my letters.

Let's understand this in proper perspective. In a single year, the number of people illegally crossing our border outnumbered the counted population in fourteen different states, in addition to Washington, DC:

STATE	POPULATION
Illegal Aliens	*1,853,528*
Alaska	710,231
Delaware	897,934
District of Columbia	601,723
Hawaii	1,360,301
Idaho	1,567,582
Maine	1,328,361
Montana	989,415
Nebraska	1,826,341
New Hampshire	1,316,470
North Dakota	672,591
Rhode Island	1,052,567
South Dakota	814,180
Vermont	625,741
West Virginia	1,852,994
Wyoming	563,626

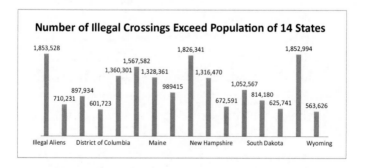

If this is anywhere near accurate, this is totally unconscionable.

There has been a slow shift in our nation. Many of us have sensed it, but the tangible evidence is becoming increasingly clear. More and more people are receiving assistance from our federal government. Our population is shifting away from a mind-set of personal responsibility to a mind-set of dependency, and the number of those actually paying to keep government going is narrowing; we can ill afford to have people coming in and out of our country without doing so in a legal manner, particularly in the volume that outpaces fourteen states and the District of Columbia.[98] Being permissive of illegal activity of any type only leads to fraud, abuse, and social costs. We can ill afford a system that says, on your first act in coming to America, "break our laws."

Sara Murray wrote a blog in the *Wall Street Journal* that was published in October 2011 and confirmed 48.5 percent of our population lived in a household that received some sort of government assistance. Since some of those must be receiving benefits that they have earned (military service benefits, retirement for government employees), I am glad the writer also included more granular data from the US Census Bureau: 34.2 percent of Americans receive benefits such as food stamps, subsidized housing, cash welfare, or Medicaid.

Murray also referenced research by the nonpartisan Tax Policy Center that estimated 46.4 percent of households will pay no federal income tax this year. That is right—*almost half of American households pay no income tax, yet almost half receive some sort of benefit.* It is not being an alarmist to sound the bell for the crisis mode when numbers like this are being published.

Our nation of laws cannot continuously function with millions of people living in the shadows, and we must resolve the continual debate of whether to educate this sector of our population. Those living in the United States illegally must resolve their status in a limited, narrow, and well-defined time frame; otherwise, the cycle never ends.

WHAT TO DO WITH THOSE WHO ARE HERE

If revamping an immigration system that has obviously failed the American rule of law, consumers, the economy, and legal immigrants wasn't hard enough, deciding what to do with the estimated 11 million–20 million people who are in the country illegally, undocumented, or what other terminology you choose to use certainly is a monumental problem of its own. In fact, many agree this is the single most complex and divisive point and is interfering with passage of legislation to attempt to remedy the remaining problems with our immigration system.

Positions on this dilemma range from providing immediate citizenship to "Round them all up and send them home" to everything in between.

The reality is that there is no solitary solution to this predicament. If citizenship were granted immediately or even as a part of the resolution, doesn't that only encourage more illegal entry? Wouldn't it perpetuate the practice of amnesty by our federal government and encourage future generations of immigrants to disregard our laws? Wouldn't it say "Don't worry, you will achieve citizenship by breaking our laws rather than keeping them, and it will be easier and better and more attainable than through the established legal means"?

For limited government advocates, building a system of law enforcement to "round up" the millions of people would be a monumental undertaking, lead to unconscionable infringement of rights of legal citizens and residents, and be so costly as to make even the big spenders in Washington blush.

Surely Americans can do better. Surely that same American will that put a man on the moon, the American fortitude that defeated Communism in the Soviet Union, and the American spirit that has nurtured and encouraged our free enterprise system is still alive and well in this generation. I believe we can and I believe we must find a solution to securing our border and reforming our failed immigration system. We should not allow this progressively dangerous problem to persist.

Why should we give this unresolved problem, only to fester and become more poisonous, to the next generation to inherit? We should not.

Reforms in 1924, 1965, and 1986 have not gotten us to where we need to be as a nation. Let us do it right in the second decade of the twenty-first century.

Action to resolve the status of those here illegally:

- Implement a Penalty not Pardon policy— *amnesty is not an option.*
- The undocumented population must undergo deportation; or
- The undocumented population can pursue a temporary six-month conditional status with the following strict requirements:
    - Come forward, fully report, and pay a fine. The fine must be meaningful, not a

slap on the wrist. Judicial Watch reported in 2011 a Tunisian imam paid $5,000 to get smuggled across the border near San Diego from Mexico. Perhaps this amount could serve as a good starting point for the discussion about further defining *meaningful*.

- Be listed on a registry of individuals not eligible for future US citizenship; if citizenship is sought, the process must begin like everyone else seeking entry into the United States: from the country of origin.
- Submit to a criminal background check.
- During the six months, demonstrate or secure verifiable employment to gain legal resident (not citizenship) status. Demonstrate your presence in this country did not occur within the previous twenty-four months (something is needed to avoid a rush before the law is passed).
- Failure to adhere to these requirements and become fully documented will result in immediate deportation.
- This provision has a short operational timeframe and a certain deadline. It keeps intact the US economic sector that has developed from a lack of enforcement or workforce visas and provides a cost-efficient alternative to deportation for which the American taxpayer would pick up the

tab. A short timeframe, certain deadline, changes in the work visa program, and strict enforcement eliminates any incentive to come here illegally in the future as this is a one-time option.

I recognize there will be debate, pros, and cons on the above conditions. There should be. Many of the elements have been discussed for years. Regardless of your opinion on the details, I hope you would agree this method says "If it is work you want and these are services our country needs, then the above scenario gets us started in a manner that can accomplish our country's objectives. If it is citizenship you want or amnesty you want to offer, this doesn't do it for you." Pushing amnesty does not help our country resolve the problem of our insecure border or our immigration system.

Employers and businesses must have a role in the reformation of our immigration system. They must verify their employees to ensure legal status through an improved electronic verification system that reduces the employer burden and their role in enforcing our immigration laws.

Through a proper documentation process, we can move those living in the shadows into a legitimate status, and our economy, society, and law-based system of governance will benefit from the elimination of a secondary market and society that is undermining the promise of America.

A MINOR ISSUE

In regard to minors who were brought to the United States as minors by their parents, well, this is a hard one. You certainly should not create an incentive to bring children to the United States for citizenship (nor for people to come here so their children will be born as US citizens, which is a whole other debate). What complicates this, in my mind, is this: children who were brought to America with their parents when they were three, five, or ten. These children have been enrolled in school and lived in the United States practically their whole lives. I am thinking about children who have English as their only language; they know of no other country. I think any rational person would have to conclude that in these children's minds, the United States of America is their home.

It seems reasonable to have an option for the minors who were victims themselves to remain in our country legally while eliminating incentives for continued abuse of our immigration laws.

One option is for individuals who, as minors, were brought to the United States by their parents to submit to the six-month grace opportunity outlined. Minors could initiate the process within a year of the date reform is enacted or upon turning eighteen years of age. Failure to do so forfeits the opportunity for permanent residency and any potential for future citizenship.

This is based on the American tradition that children cannot inherit the guilt of their parent's crime, but they must accept responsibility for their own actions and become contributing and documented adults. This proposal is also consistent with our American criminal justice system that seeks to establish accountability but recognizes minors should be treated differently than adults. For those that suggest this option would be amnesty, I ask, can amnesty be given if no crime has been committed? I mean, a child in a car seat of a bank robbery getaway car has committed no crime; they are a victim themselves and would never be charged along with the driver. No crime, no amnesty.

M: MANDATE COUNTRY OF ORIGIN APPLICATION FOR US CITIZENSHIP

Mandates are generally not a good thing. When it comes to unfunded mandates, government must not walk away; it should *run*! Unfunded mandates from the federal government to the states, from the states to the counties, cities, and schools are and should be a major point of contention because the practice has driven up government spending and has oftentimes been an excuse for a governmental body to do more than is required under the claimed duress of "unfunded mandate."

When it comes to securing our border, our federal government must grow a backbone. The president and members of Congress must clearly define a path forward for our country and must provide certainty in the way the United States is going to do business. The public servants who process visa requests or detain drug dealers and states frustrated with fighting for a way to manage the chaos need relief.

When it comes to border security and immigration, a mandate is something our government should do. The federal government must mandate country of origin application for US citizenship; this is the only way to discourage future illegal entries. Without this requirement, we would head down the corridor to amnesty again and continue the perpetual problems that have been plaguing our immigration system for decades.

Why should reform come at the expense of immigrants migrating legally under our current system? We should anticipate poor results and continued chaos when we say with our policies, "Don't worry, you broke our laws, and now we will reward you." Any parent knows the danger and mischief this type of philosophy breeds.

Our country should be pro *legal* immigration. If you want to become a citizen of the United States of America, we welcome you. We have a legal process for applying for citizenship. If that process needs to be modernized, better equipped, more technologically advanced, and market based, that is a debate and discussion we should have. However, doing away with our immigration laws and thumbing our nose at our system of government by rewarding illegal behavior simply sends the wrong message, one that only will make illegal entry into our country worse than it already is today. It also would continue to provide cover to the drug cartels as they use the situation to their benefit.

In taking a stand against amnesty, let it be known to all peoples far and wide that from this day forth, to be eligible for citizenship in the United States of America, an applicant must apply from their country of origin. Let it be known that America is the land of the free, the home of the brave, and a welcoming hostess to people who will abide by our laws.

Let it be known we expect and demand all others to abide by our laws as well. Let it be known the determined spirit that built this country out of a wilderness, out of economic and religious persecution from foreign powers, and out of an amalgamation of people with diverse cultures and economic status will carry the banner of freedom forward and will not sacrifice the foundation of American liberty for political expediency or rewards of power.

R: REFORM THE FAILED VISA SYSTEM FOR GUEST WORKERS AND INTERNATIONAL DAY LABORERS

The Texas Department of Agriculture has one of the most diverse missions of any state agency. From weights and measures (for example, ensuring the accuracy of the scales at your local grocery store and the quality of the gasoline you put in your car) to plant health and safety to economic development to rural health initiatives to administering the nation's largest school lunch program—the list goes on.

From the beginning of the agency back in 1907, its main function has been to promote production agriculture in the state of Texas, which means ensuring those involved in the many links of the agricultural production chain have the opportunity to grow, harvest, and move crops and livestock to market. Bearing arms to secure our borders and administering a guest worker system is *not* among the department's duties. Assisting constituents who suffer from bad policy is our responsibility and one we take seriously, particularly when people's lives and livelihoods are at stake.

In the previous chapters, you have read about the damage our farmers, ranchers, and rural landowners face due to the violence along our porous and insecure border. Our farmers and ranchers are also negatively impacted by our current immigration system. Without workers, the fields are not harvested, livestock doesn't ship to market, and you and I don't have access to medicines and other household products that include agricultural products at their base.

One agricultural company just made a $45 million capital investment in Texas and cannot find the employees to meet the company's needs, even though they pay well above minimum wage. The oil and gas sector is also struggling to find qualified employees.

The US immigration system is complex, and honestly, there is little wonder why workers and employers circumvent the system. Just look at the types of visas that must be deciphered to legally work, study, and visit in the United States.

- B-1 Business Visa
- B-2 Tourist Visa
- E-1/E-2 Visa
- F-1 Student Visa
- J-1 Exchange Visitor Visa
- H-1B Visa
- H-2A Visa

- K-1 Fiancé(e)/Fiancé Visa
- TN NAFTA Work Visa
- Tourist Visa Extension[99]

As I travel across our state, economic development is a topic I'm often asked to address. And often when speaking to the men and women who run the small businesses that are the engine of our economy, the conversations evolve and eventually focus on workforce; our businesses don't have enough qualified and dependable workers to grow. This dilemma could not be more pronounced than in agriculture.

American agriculture usually uses the H-2A visa. Searching a US government administered site revealed the chart reprinted below.

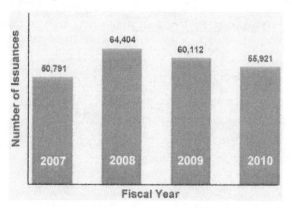

Source: Immigrationdirect.com

- Chart represents the number of H-2A visas issued according to the year.
- The H-2A visa program allows US employers to bring foreign nationals to the United States

to fill temporary agricultural jobs for which US workers are not available.

- H-2A nonimmigrant classification applies to foreigners seeking to perform agricultural labor or services of a temporary or seasonal nature in the United States on a temporary basis.

There are a few observations I hope you gathered from this chart.

First, the visas granted for fiscal years 2008–2010 average about sixty thousand per year. Do you really think there are only sixty thousand noncitizen or legal workers helping with the massive agriculture industry in America? If agriculture only needed sixty thousand visas, I don't think you would have the outcry from the industry for reform.

Second, notice that two of the chart explanations discuss the "temporary or seasonal nature" of the H-2A visa. Ironically, the agriculture industry has more than seasonal needs. There is nothing seasonal about a dairy industry that requires year-round labor. I like milk year-round; my cereal (another agricultural product!) just doesn't taste right without it. There is nothing temporary about a feedlot operation, an important segment of the Texas $7-plus billion cattle industry. We like to eat American beef, chicken, and pork year-round.

Another interesting chart pertinent to the discussion is the number of H-2B visas approved.

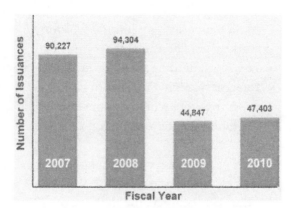

Source: Immigrationdirect.com

- Chart represents the number of H-2B visas issued according to the year.
- The H-2B visa is one of the only visa categories that authorizes unskilled laborers to work in the United States. For this reason, this category is highly in demand for individuals who may not be eligible to apply for any other US visa.
- Many US employers rely on H-2B visa program to fill temporary or seasonal needs that would be impossible to fill with US workers.
- Employer-sponsored visa category.
- Special immigrant visa category.

According to our federal policy makers, the H-2A and H-2B are both designed essentially for "unskilled laborers" (farmers would argue, rightfully so, that it takes skill to work in modern agriculture). Both visas are for "temporary or seasonal" needs.

Math time again.

For 2010, H-2A visas totaled roughly 56,000 and H-2B 48,000 (rounded up). This equals 104,000 people.

Now, remember the estimate of people who came into the United States illegally based on Border Patrol numbers and a little math exercise? That number was 1,853,528.

Dividing 104,000 legally approved visas by the 1,853,528 who entered illegally yields a factor of almost 18. Said another way, our market-based system of supply and demand requires eighteen times the workforce provided by our workforce visas! Time for reform, don't you think?

Now, one may argue (or many may argue) that examining or comparing only the H-2A and H-2B visas is not a fair analysis. However, these are the categories that focus mainly on unskilled workers. I have a hard time believing many people risk life and limb running through the wild country of South Texas or the dry and remote areas of New Mexico and Arizona for a desk job. It just isn't happening that way.

Farmers and ranchers are independent, tough, sometimes stubborn, but never bashful when they have had enough. They have been speaking out loudly about the need for reforming our failed guest worker programs. The immigration-direct.com website posted an article about changes in the visa system. I added emphasis and a few details in parentheses to provide perspective on how this visa, designed for agriculture, relates to the broader immigration debate.

New H-2B Rules Provide Better Security for
Workers and Employers
Thu, Feb 23 10:14 AM

A new H-2B visas rule change may make
it easier for undocumented workers to find
employment *[Talk about a wink-and-a nod
policy! Law generally provides that those who are
here without the proper visa and are undocumented
are supposed to be deported!]*, according to the
United States Department of Labor.

The department announced a new final rule
on February 21 that will give temporary foreign
workers greater access to jobs and worker's
rights.

Recent statistics show that the number of
H-2B visas approved has drastically declined in
recent years. While more than 94,000 of these
US visas were approved in 2008, this number
dropped to less than 45,000 in 2009—less than
half of the previous year's total. While rates
have increased slightly in recent years, numbers
have still stayed below 50,000. The current
program is limited to 66,000 visas per year.
*[I hope you're wondering why, when 1.8 million
people are coming illegally, do we have a system
that is capped at 66,000?]*

The article goes on to discuss employer influence on
the new rule:

The rule is in large part written through the
comments of employers and worker advocates,

who assisted in drafting the final rule. Slated to come into effect on April 23, the new rule also requires the creation of a national registry posting all H-2B job postings. Giving both workers and employers greater flexibility, the new rule also improves the recruitment process as well as the length of time workers can be employed. Former employees will be hired when available as well under the new set of rules, so a certain sense of job security can also come with the program.

The article explains that according to reports from across the country, the H-2A visa is in need of reform:

> While the visa program offers a legal alternative for hiring foreign help in agricultural work, current processing for the visas can take months for approval, *[You and I both know businesses don't have time to wait for employees. You land a new contract and you have to produce… not wait for the federal government to process your request for workers.]* making the program extremely inefficient for those working within a certain time range for growing seasons. *[It is no wonder farmers and ranchers are frustrated, nor should we be surprised that people are flocking to our jobs illegally rather than trying to use the system.]*[101]

I'm sorry if reading that press release and my added commentary made you tired. I am exhausted. I am frustrated. Is there any wonder we have a mess on our hands?

Rectifying this critical component of workforce development and keeping our economy going to meet market demands requires action:

- The visa-application process must be streamlined and deadlines strictly enforced.
- Policies must recognize industries that need visa workers on an annual basis need a longer-term solution. An annual emergency worker program is just a tax on businesses that can't find a workforce.
- Guest worker allotments must be increased and be based on market demands and not arbitrary quotas.
- Reforming our guest worker programs is critical and can start by simplifying and bringing together all programs into one and recognizing the needs of agriculture, service, and construction to provide them a legal, documented workforce.
- Technology must be used to enforce the penalties for overstaying a visa and for shortening the timeframe for the application and approval process.

Unfortunately, no one has a monopoly on good ideas when it comes to reforming our guest worker system. If they did, we could implement this wonderful idea, and the critics would be few. As it stands, we must continue the dialogue on the most reasonable course of action.

Forbes published a guest post by Sean Rust, law and public policy scholar at Temple University Beasley School of Law, entitled "Why Market-Based Immigration Is America's Best Bet." Rust lays out a five-point plan, which includes allowing mobility for the visa and requiring the people seeking visas to actually purchase them with the cost tied to the length of stay.[102]

P: PORTS MUST BE MODERNIZED

Gateways, portals, entryways—our sea, air, and land ports are the nerve centers of commerce. In agriculture, we discuss frequently that 96 percent of the world's consumers live outside the borders of the United States of America.[103] Accessing these markets, and in turn receiving the products shipped to America that American consumers demand, is indispensable for a stable and growing economy.

It doesn't take a rocket scientist or brain surgeon to know that the least resistant path to drug trafficking is through rural, remote portions of our border. These areas are sparsely populated, and law enforcement has a difficult time patrolling the vast geography and rugged terrain. This is where our farmers and ranchers live and work and where they have been demanding greater assistance. But in being consistent with the theme that there is no silver bullet to addressing the multiple issues surrounding border security and our failed guest worker programs, one has to look at the ports along our southern border through which our legal trade and commerce is focused.

The *Seattle Times* printed an article on October 8, 2011, that contained this salient statement and conclusion:

> After a decade of record deportations, critics argue, it has become even harder to separate the two groups that now define the border: professional criminals and experienced migrants motivated by family ties in the United States.
>
> "If you think drug dealers and terrorists are much more dangerous than maids and gardeners, then we should get as many visas as possible to those people, so we can focus on the real threat," said David Shirk, director of the Transborder Institute at the University of San Diego. "Widening the gates would strengthen the walls."[104]

Gate widening has been a consistent theme for many of the communities along our southern border whose economic success is dependent upon active and legal trade with our southern partner. Private businesses throughout our country that deal directly with imports from and exports to Mexico have consistently repeated the need to modernize and improve the ports of entry to facilitate the large volume of trade that exists with one of our most valuable trading partners.

In 2010, the North American Center for Transborder Studies (NACTS) at Arizona State University published "Realizing the Full Value of Crossborder Trade with Mexico." The study makes a strong case for enhancing our commitment to trade with Mexico and leveraging the economic opportunities for mutual success.

The study shows the number of major crossings (or ports) that facilitate trade between our two countries. They are located at the following cities: Nogales, Calexico E, Otay, Santa Teresa, Brownsville, Del Rio, Eagle Pass, El Paso, Laredo, and Hidalgo.[105]

Reflecting on the benefit to America from both exports and imports, the authors reported the following:

> Exports clearly create jobs, but what is less apparent is that *exports rely on imports*. When US firms build and produce things together with firms in Mexico, it is imperative for them to get key components across the border as fast as possible back into their facilities.
>
> The sooner they are in, the sooner they may continue to move along the supply chain until they reach the consumer and create a profit for the U.S. firm and the economy. In a just-in-time business environment, the company relies on an efficient process at the border in order to get numerous key components shipped rapidly from Mexico.[106]

If America desires to continue the economic benefits that arise from trade with Mexico, economic experts and policy analysts agree a dynamic port system that facilitates legal trade and eliminates illegal activity is vital to our future.

CORRUPTION, PUBLIC OR PRIVATE, MUST NOT BE TOLERATED

A nalyzing our border security and immigration problems is not simple. There are many political, social, and economic factors that have given rise to our current environment where cartel violence and illegal immigration are condoned and even encouraged by some in the governments of Mexico and the United States. A full discussion of these issues is beyond the scope of my intent in writing *Broken Borders, Broken Promises*. However, I would be remiss in completely ignoring them.

TOO MANY BAD EXAMPLES

Enron executives, Martha Stewart, Bernie Madoff, and former governors Rod Blagojevich (Illinois) and Edwin Edwards (Louisiana) are all examples of leaders who forgot what leadership is all about and put profits above integrity and self-gratification above their neighbor. This is not what the American dream is all about, and whether in private business affairs or in public service, violators of this trust must be prosecuted to the fullest extent of the law if we are to demand honesty and integrity in the affairs of man.

Lonesome Dove by Larry McMurtry is a classic tale of the struggles of settling in the West. You may not be a fan of Westerns (I watched them as a young child on Saturday afternoons with my grandmother—great memories), but you hopefully appreciate the sense of justice and commitment to doing the right thing that was usually conveyed. There are many powerful scenes in *Lonesome Dove*, but one in particular stands out when conveying the drive for accountability.

Jake Spoon had ridden with the heroes and stars of the series, Captain Augustus McCrae and Captain Woodrow Call, two former Texas Rangers. But Jake had fallen in with a bad lot of men who were stealing horses (an offense that carried the penalty of hanging) and were killing farmers. Things didn't go well for Jake when Gus and Woodrow caught up to the gang of thieves and dispensed frontier justice.

> Jake Spoon: Oh, you don't need to tie me up, Newt. Hell, I didn't kill anybody. I just fell in with these boys to get through the Territory. Hell, I was gonna leave 'em first chance I got!
>
> Gus McCrae: I wish you had taken that chance a little earlier, Jake. A man who'll go along with five killings is takin' his leave a little slow.
>
> Gus McCrae: You know how it works, Jake. You ride with an outlaw, you die with an outlaw. I'm sorry you crossed the line.
>
> Jake Spoon: I didn't see no line, Gus. I was just tryin' to get through the territory without getting scalped.[107]

Poor Jake didn't see a line, and he crossed over into bad company and ended up hanging with the rest of the killers he was a part of and supported.

We need bright lines of good and bad and accountability when those lines are crossed. Any official or private citizen needs to know corruption will not be tolerated. Public officials and law enforcement should be even held to a higher standard because they have taken an oath to protect the public and uphold the public trust. Friends and neighbors put their confidence in them and offer support and respect as they carry out their duties. This is not something to be taken lightly, and those who cross the line should be brought to modern justice. We have too many examples of corruption deteriorating the quality of life for society.

Mexican president Felipe Calderon took what many Americans would consider extreme measures by militarizing the drug war. Part of the reason the Mexican military has been engaged in confronting the drug cartels is because the cartels infiltrated and corrupted the local police and officials.[108]

With the summer 2012 election of Enrique Pena Nieto, all eyes are anxiously awaiting what the new president's course of action will be to deal with the corruption, killing, and takeover of towns and regions of Mexico. President Pena Nieto has suggested there will be a shift more focused on *protecting ordinary citizens from gangs.*[109] His talk of a shifting strategy and lack of specificity of his anti–crime-fighting tactics has many wondering what will be the consequences to the United States, as is reflected in an Associated Press article.

That ambiguity has fed fears at home and abroad that Pena Nieto might look the other way if cartels smuggle drugs northward without creating violence in Mexico. Many analyst wonder if Pena Nieto is holding back politically sensitive details of his plans, or simply doesn't know yet how he'll prosecute the next stage of Mexico's drug war.[110]

The Texas Department of Public Safety (DPS) manages a public corruption unit to help ensure the integrity of our law enforcement system. DPS's work should be commended. Their website offers a simple warning of the ominous statement of the cartel intentions.

Mexican cartels are adept at corrupting law enforcement officers in Mexico, and they also seek to corrupt public officials in the United States.

Corruption, like cartel violence, transcends the border. Right here, in our own state, many have crossed the line.

Since October 1, 2004, 127 CBP employees have been arrested or indicted for acts of corruption, including drug smuggling, alien smuggling, money laundering, and conspiracy; of those arrests, 95 percent are considered mission-compromising acts of corruption:

- Former Cameron County sheriff's deputy Jesus A. Longoria was sentenced in March 2011 to fifty-seven months in prison after pleading guilty to attempting to allow weapons to be trafficked into Mexico.

- Former Sullivan City police chief Hernan Guerra was sentenced in 2011 to ten years in prison for his involvement in a drug-trafficking organization.

- Former Zapata County justice of the peace Manuel Martinez and former South Texas Violent Crimes Task Force investigator Jose Amaro pleaded guilty in August 2007 for extorting money from drug traffickers in exchange for using their official positions to ensure the undetected passage of drug traffickers and their drug shipments through Zapata County between June 2006 and November 2006.

- Former Texas Department of Criminal Justice guard Alejandro Smith pleaded guilty in August 2011 to possessing heroin with the intent to distribute.

- Former Reeves County jailer Raul Garcia Jr. pleaded guilty in 2007 for possession with intent to distribute a controlled substance.

- Former Starr County sheriff Reymundo Guerra was sentenced to five years and four months in federal prison in August 2009 for helping Gulf Cartel operatives move marijuana and cocaine through his border county.

- Former Laredo police officer Pedro Martinez III was sentenced to seventy-eight months in federal prison in August 2011 for conspiracy to possess with intent to distribute more than five kilograms of cocaine.

- Former DPS trooper Jesus Rafael Larrazolo was sentenced to eighty-seven months in federal prison in November 2009 for possession with intent to distribute fifty-seven pounds of cocaine.[111]

Fighting corruption is vital to preserving our democracy, protecting our borders, and securing our communities. It is also vital to ensuring families can raise their children, go to work, and run their businesses. Corruption leading to societal disruption has taken a tremendous toll on the regional economy that suffers such daily life-threatening situations as they do in the northern Mexican states.

While the overall Mexican economy has outpaced the United States over the last few years, the dishonesty and violence has hampered activities and overall growth despite the claims of some Mexican government officials.

"If there were no violence, the Mexican economy would have grown 1 percent above the rates of the past few years," said Jorge Sicilia, chief economist for

BBVA Spanish bank, a major financial force operating in Mexico.[112]

Other statements reflect the consequences to the regions facing the brunt of the infestation of the cartel activities:

> The Canacintra national manufacturing industry chamber recently estimated that up to 10,000 small and medium enterprises had shut down during 2010 in the areas most badly affected by the drug violence.
>
> Many of them had suffered extortion or threats from criminals who demanded the payment of a "fee" for their security.[113]

We must remain steadfast in our efforts to maintain high ethical standards, honesty, and integrity in our officials and society and hold firm in opposition to those who cross the line.

OUR FUTURE IS ON THE LINE

Remember reading *Animal Farm* by George Orwell in school? It struck me how the young were indoctrinated, and some were pulled aside for "special" training. How the facts were distorted and the circumstances changed in order for the "pigs" to gain and keep control.

Sending the right message to children who will be the next generation of decision makers is key to building a better future. That is why many in Texas have joined together with me to create the Grow Texas Foundation. Grow Texas is a scholarship program funded solely from private contributions and is dedicated to supporting students who value, understand, and appreciate the role that agriculture and leadership plays in our state and national economy.

Many youth organizations exist that help to ensure our children receive the proper training and right message about the importance of work, integrity, honesty, responsibility, and the essential aspects of our country's free enterprise system. The 4H Foundation and National FFA Association are two that continue to create opportunities for the youth of our day. They rely on thousands of adult volunteers who give generously of their time and money to support these students. The adults who serve know the talent of these young minds and seek to cultivate them into prosperous and contributing adults. These organizations have even led to philanthropists like Dick Wallrath to create their own endowments. The Richard Wallrath Educational Foundation sponsored the production of the 2012 movie *Deep in the Heart*, which tells of the personal demons Wallrath overcame to give back millions for youth scholarships. My own life was greatly enriched by agriculture teachers, Harold Gilbert and Tom Hill, along with my government teacher, Marley Styner, who carried me to many places in order to compete and learn.

Drug cartel leaders also recognize the ability of the young, but their intent and purpose is more nefarious. From the Texas Department of Public Safety website, they have identified trends that are frightening, if you care about kids.

> Mexican cartels recruit Texas youth to traffic drugs across the border. The Texas border region represents 9.7% of the state's population, yet this region has 19.2% of the state's juvenile felony drug referrals and 21.8% of the state's juvenile felony gang referrals.
>
> In October 2011, the Texas Department of Public Safety (DPS) apprehended a 12-year-old boy in a border county driving a stolen pickup truck containing more than 800 pounds of marijuana.
>
> In another border county, more than 25 juveniles have been arrested for drug trafficking within the past year.

We all wish and hope to believe these are isolated incidents. They are not. When accompanying Border

Patrol and navigating the Rio Grande, young people were pointed out to me who were suggested to be scouts radioing back to the cartel members our activities and time of the patrol.

Securing our borders is more than about controlling who comes in and out of our country, which is decisively important all by itself. It is also about creating a better environment for the children of our nation. Securing our border is our responsibility. One need look no farther than the statistics signaling our children are in danger.

SENDING THE RIGHT SIGNAL IS A PART OF WINNING

Dr. Frank Luntz has been a part of many winning campaigns and initiatives. His book *Words That Work* should be mandatory reading for anyone whose job it is to communicate with the public. Actually, the tips and concepts Dr. Luntz lays out are good for business, volunteer organizations, and particularly getting along with teenagers!

The subtitle pretty much says it all: *It's not what you say, it's what people hear.*

How words are understood can lead to a peaceful resolution or only serve to heighten the engagement (engagement here not being the romance variety).

In 2011, reading the *Dallas Morning News* in early to mid-April and coming across the Mexican ambassador to the United States letter to the editor made me spew my coffee and elevated my blood pressure to an unhealthy status. His complete letter is reprinted below.

On Mexico and violence

By
Dallasnews.com/letters
5:37 p.m.on Mon., Apr. 11, 2011

Choose labels carefully
Re: "Let's call México's Cartels what they are: terrorists," Friday Editorials.

The editorial should be better headed "Let's Call Mexico's cartels what they are: very violent, well-financed transnational criminal organizations." These transnational criminal organizations, which operate in both our countries, are not terrorist organizations. They are very violent criminal groups that are well-structured and well-financed. They pursue a single goal. They want to maximize their profits and do what most business do: hostile takeovers and pursue mergers and acquisitions. They use violence to protect their business from other competitors as well as from our two governments' efforts to roll them back. There is no political motivation or agenda whatsoever beyond their attempt to defend their illegal business.

Misunderstanding the challenge we face leads to wrong policies and bad policy making. If you label these organizations as terrorist, you will have to start calling drug consumers in the U.S. "financiers of terrorist organizations" and gun dealers "providers of material support to terrorists." Otherwise, you really sound as if you want to have your cake and eat it too. That's why I would underscore that the editorial page should be careful what it advocates for.

—Arturo Sarukhan
Ambassador of Mexico to the US
Washington, DC [114]

Mr. Ambassador, please do not give these people who resort to beheadings and dismemberment and hangings any semblance of a business operation. Are they organized? Of course. Do they implement complex distribution systems and have well-developed financial schemes and recruitment mechanisms? Obviously. But to give the appearance of defending them by saying they are businessmen just downright sends the wrong message to them and to those whose efforts we rely upon to win this battle. Read Dr. Luntz's book; please know your words matter!

My public response to Ambassador Sarukhan was published as a letter to the editor in the *Dallas Morning News* a few days later.

Ambassador's label inaccurate

By
Dallasnews.com/letters
5:23 p.m.on Thu., Apr. 14, 2011

Re: "Choose labels carefully," by Arturo Sarukhan, Tuesday Letters.

I was stunned to see the Ambassador of Mexico argue drug cartels are not terrorists, but merely "criminal organizations" that simply want "to maximize their profits." To argue over labeling is one thing. To insinuate the drug cartels are like any other business and to metaphorically compare them to entrepreneurs is shocking and tragically irresponsible. As The Dallas Morning News accurately put it, the drug cartels are terrorist organizations defined not by an ideology, but by tactics of brutality and fear. It's inconceivable this appointed leader would dismiss a threat that is tearing apart his nation. A person of Sarukhan's status should be more careful than to make such ludicrous parallels between business and terrorism.

The violent perpetrators who are filling mass graves with victims, beheading them and burning them alive are not simply criminal businessmen. They are terrorists. The violent realities are occurring right here in Texas and other border states as is documented on our website www.protectyourTexasborder.com but are being ignored by the current administration.

Sarukhan's comments are reprehensible, and we should demand a public retraction. If not, the United States should send him packing by rescinding his diplomatic status in our country.

—Todd Staples
Texas Agriculture Commissioner
Austin, TX[115]

TEXAS BORDER REGION IS DIVERSE...
AND BIG... AND PROSPEROUS

Fifteen counties stretch along the Rio Grande as a border with our southern neighbor (Dimmit is just shy of actually touching it but, for all purposes, is a border county). According to the 2010 census numbers, the total population for these counties totals almost 2.5 million people. These are very important counties to the Texas and US economy. A few statistics shown below highlight the agricultural relevance of these Texas border counties.

- The fifteen counties along the Texas border with Mexico include nearly 8,200 farms and ranches covering more than 15 million acres.
- Texas border farms and ranches contribute significantly to the fruit, vegetable, and beef provided to consumers across the state and nation.
- The Texas border counties account for nearly half of the state's fruit and vegetable production.
- Farms and ranches in Texas border counties generate over $700 million in agricultural sales annually, making them critical to the economic health of the region.
- Texas border counties are the leading gateway for US trade with Mexico, our second largest trading partner in the world.

- Agricultural exports from Texas to Mexico totaled nearly $1.4 billion in 2010.
- The twenty-seven counties that form the US border with Mexico (including fifteen in Texas) include nearly 21,000 farms and ranches covering 23 million acres.
- The US border counties generate almost $5 billion in agricultural sales annually.[116]

What these statistics don't say is that of the 1,241 miles that separates Texas and Mexico, 93 percent is estimated to be unincorporated and largely rural.

Texas cities over 20,000 in population considered on this route include the following:

City	2010 Population
El Paso	649,121
Del Rio	35,591
Eagle Pass	26,248
Laredo	236,091
Mission	77,058
McAllen	129,877
Pharr	70,400
Brownsville	175,027

These eight cities alone have a population of just shy of 1.4 million people who live right on or a stone's throw from the border. And this is the population just within the corporate boundaries.

These are vibrant, growing, and dynamic communities. They have a tremendous economic impact on our state and national economy. Ports of entry in and near these communities provide for the flow of legal trade and commerce on a daily basis—business that is essential to the economic health and wellbeing of our nation.

Higher education opportunities abound and range from the University of Texas–El Paso to Texas A&M International–Laredo to University of Texas–Brownsville, with a host of other colleges and universities mixed between. Employment opportunities range from manufacturing to medicine and from distribution and finance to research. They are open for business; come visit. I do frequently and enjoy the many fine restaurants and lodging that is available.

Some community leaders are frustrated with the talk of border violence because many actually never see it because it doesn't cross their property. Reading an account of a rancher who chased off a gang of men robbing an outbuilding on their ranch doesn't mean that you will find that every day or that it will occur inside the corporate limits of our cities. But it happens on an all-too-frequent basis in the rural, remote stretches of the southern border of the United States of America.

While every major city in America today has a certain element of gang activity and crime, the impact on the rural areas is different. Cities have public streets and are more densely populated. They have city police departments and neighborhood watch groups. The rural farms and ranches have vast and wide-open areas where there is no public access, well, legal public access anyway.

HOW DO YOU PAY FOR MORE BORDER SECURITY?

Paying for a government program? Don't you wish this question would have been asked and answered long before this point in our nation's history?

We are truly at a crisis when it comes to our indebtedness. One need to only look at Greece, Portugal, Spain, or Italy to see how massive unchecked government spending can weaken your independence as a country and threaten its financial solvency.

I think it is fair to say a high national debt weakens our national security as it limits our options defensively.

The Heritage Foundation chronicled the most recent debt accumulation in its document titled "Don't Raise the Debt Limit Without Getting Spending Under Control," Backgrounder #2549, dated April 21, 2011.

- By Act of June 28, 2002, Congress raised the debt limit to $6.4 trillion.
- By Act of May 27, 2003, Congress raised the debt limit to $7.384 trillion.
- By Act of November 19, 2004, Congress raised the debt limit to $8.184 trillion.
- By Act of March 20, 2006, Congress raised the debt limit to $8.965 trillion.
- By Act of September 29, 2007, Congress raised the debt limit to $9.815 trillion.

- By section 3083 of the Act of July 30, 2008, a 259-page law known as the Housing and Economic Recovery Act of 2008, Congress raised the debt limit to $10.615 trillion.
- By section 122 of the Act of October 3, 2008, a 168-page law known as the Emergency Economic Stabilization Act of 2008, Congress raised the debt limit to $11.315 trillion.
- By section 1604 of the Act of February 17, 2009, a 406-page law known as the American Recovery and Reinvestment Act of 2009, Congress raised the debt limit to $12.104 trillion.
- By Act of December 28, 2009, Congress raised the debt limit to $12.394 trillion.
- Finally, by Act of February 12, 2010, Congress raised the debt limit to its current amount of $14.294 trillion. The Act included some budget process reforms.[117]

We know the ceiling has been raised even higher since this report by Heritage, but here is the point: The doubling of the debt, the phenomenal and explosive growth, in less than a ten-year period should, without a doubt, persuade the American people to question the spending of every red cent by Congress and any administration, Democrat or Republican.

Heritage goes on to call for the urgent reduction in our debt and proposes a three-step process.

> As federal borrowing approaches the current debt limit of $14.294 trillion, the Speaker and the Minority Leader of the House of

Representatives and the Majority and Minority Leaders of the Senate, supported by strong majorities in the House and Senate, must reach agreement to accomplish three things to put the country on a path to financial responsibility: (1) cut current spending, (2) restrict future spending, and (3) fix the budget process.

Relief from the debt limit makes sense only if that relief is an integral part of a plan to drive down spending and borrowing so that the country lives within its means. Although Congress must make substantial cuts in current and future spending, the cuts should come in non-security spending, as the United States needs to fully fund defense of America and its interests around the globe.

A critical element is captured in the last sentence about the US needing to be fully capable to attend to its defense duties around the globe. I would expand upon that to highlight the inclusion of its defense duties domestically.

Spending is a matter of priorities. Will we, as a nation, allow for more Solyndra projects at a time when we can ill afford deficit spending to add to the debt? The General Services Administration spending $823,000 for a training conference in Las Vegas doesn't demonstrate federal government leaders are very serious about reducing the waste. As Bill O'Reilly pointed out on the *O'Reilly Factor*, the spending for appetizers was about $4 per shrimp! Four bucks will still buy you a great hamburger in Texas!

We must be efficient in our government spending, and that includes for both domestic and global defense purposes. We must also make these spending items our first priority.

US senator Tom Coburn, MD (R-OK) releases a list of top government wasteful spending projects. I won't attempt to relist them here, but surely a majority of Americans could agree that performing an undeniably constitutional duty and defending our border from transnational criminal organizations would take precedence over many of the current discretionary spending items.

WHY DON'T WE JUST LEGALIZE DRUGS?

This continues to be a resounding theme: legalize drugs, do away with the underground economy, tax the trade, and take the incentive away from the organized criminal activity and violence that defines the drug trafficking today. Think of the money that will be saved from lowering the need for intervention, enforcement, and incarceration.

Former Mexican president Vicente Fox is an advocate for such. I heard him personally suggest it at a dinner I hosted in Fort Worth for agriculture commissioners, secretaries, and directors from Canada, Mexico, and the United States. Fox has been a good leader for Mexico, a strong advocate for advanced trade for our North American countries, and a strong ally for the United States at a time when world opinion has sometimes been less than favorable. I couldn't disagree with him more on this issue.

What should we legalize? Marijuana? Heroin? How about cocaine or methamphetamines? Why do we have any laws at all?

Now, you might argue that if the sale and distribution of drugs were decriminalized, the violence would go away as well. It just seems there is an element here that cannot be reasoned with under any circumstances.

Legalization would certainly increase dependency, and to those who suggest otherwise, I think they just don't understand or choose to ignore basic supply and demand and pricing issues, not to mention marketing opportunities to drive product. Does the state need to sanction harmful substances and say "Okay, we give up"? Is the correct policy to say we're conquered? That we will concede defeat to those who have kidnapped and killed children, who have murdered our law enforcement officers, and who have flouted our laws? No, quitting just isn't me.

Some may say, "Just be smart about it. Look at the cost savings. Look at the tax revenue that will come in as a result."

I agree the war on drugs has gotten derailed, and now we face a drug war on America. But look at legalized prescription drugs. Is there not a major problem with addiction and abuse that most recently claimed the life of a beautiful and talented singer, Whitney Houston, in a tragic manner?

"If you can't beat 'em, join 'em." This slogan just does not apply.

You want to really solve this problem of illegal narcotics flowing into our country? How about starting with parents being responsible role models for their children? Teach children the value of human life. Educate this upcoming generation about how illegal narcotics have ruined so many lives. And, how about Hollywood stop glamorizing the lifestyle of those that make a living shortening the lives of others?

AMERICANS HAVE A HISTORY OF OVERCOMING

For the past two hundred–plus years, the United States of America has encountered numerous conflicts and trials, wars and recessions, heartaches and difficulties. Not all have been of the gravity as endured by the unprovoked attack on the Twin Towers on September 11, 2001, or the painful economic depression of the 1930s, but they were nonetheless painful and could have been eternally crippling.

Americans, however, chose to demonstrate resolve. Americans banded together to conquer strife of both regional and national proportions. *Broken Borders, Broken Promises* seeks to highlight some of the periods in our nation's history that were not our brightest moments to serve as a reminder of what all we have achieved and overcome. Collectively, people from all walks of life and varied ethnicity have built a true economic and military powerhouse, even with all of its shortcomings, that is unparalleled in today's world. I thank God for blessing these multigenerational efforts and pray for his guidance as we embark on solving the dilemmas of our day.

Many will have strong opinions about the suggestions offered herein, both for and against. I hope they express them loudly and forcefully. I hope those calling for a solution and those offering criticism will remain at the drawing board until a national solution is sketched and printed. I am optimistic Americans will demand from those who unapologetically say what they are against to step forward calmly with what they are for.

As someone who, since his early years, truly believes the tenth amendment of the United States Constitution has been ignored far beyond the imagination of our founding fathers, I am extremely sympathetic with states that have attempted to solve this border, workforce, and immigration catastrophe that now ensnares us. States are excellent resources to work on policy, and the federal government would do well to rein in its appetite and leave room for states to maneuver on a number of issues. But if there ever was an issue that demanded a national solution, this is one.

In truth, this framework being offered is a compilation of excellent work that has been conducted in my state and states around the country. It includes concepts of our congressional delegation, business trade groups, border-focused associations, landowner associations, and agricultural organizations. It includes conversations with Hispanic leaders and chambers of commerce. No single person or group has all the answers, but together, success can be achieved.

Injustice of any kind offends me. It is unjust when people fail to work and provide for themselves and their families, and it is unjust when the weak and helpless are taken advantage of. America needs more individuals to step forward and demand justice and not leave problems for someone else to handle.

APPENDIX

Statement from Texas Agriculture Commissioner Todd Staples

"A Call to Action: Narco-Terrorism's Threat to the Southern U.S. Border"

Hearing Before the House Subcommittee on Oversight, Investigations, and Management of the House Committee on Homeland Security

October 14, 2011

Thank you, Mr. Chairman and members of the committee, for the opportunity to testify before you today. I am Todd Staples, Texas Commissioner of Agriculture.

Texas Border Security: A Strategic Military Assessment documents in clear terms, we have a violently insecure, porous border, with a lack of operational control. Texas is simply calling for sufficient action–ample federal resources to secure our country. No one is blaming our national leaders for the drug cartels' seedy motives and heinous actions – but saying "our border is safer than ever" signals two dangerous messages to these narco-terrorist organizations that are infiltrating America: 1. We are satisfied with the status quo, and 2. We are not going to drive you out of business. Congressmen, the only message from a united

America should be this: We will meet any opposing force with greater force and we will not cede one inch of American soil.

This committee knows firsthand from testimony and field hearings the threats in Mexico that have been well documented as well as our law enforcement and foreign aid efforts at the national, state, and local levels to counter these violent transnational criminal organizations. At this very moment a critical industry to our national security is under increasing attack. Texas farmers and ranchers along the U.S.-Mexico border are regularly becoming victims of intimidation, aggression and outright violence by armed trespassers that often have direct ties to Mexico's drug cartels. With alarming frequency, Texans along the border are subjected to physical harassment, illegal trespassing, property damage, theft and the illegal trafficking of people and drugs on their property.

I come to you today to say we must not minimize the actions of terrorists. This border assessment tells the stories of farmers, ranchers and rural landowners who have been victims of violence; who witness grim atrocities on a far too frequent basis; and generally live in fear of those who cross their land day and night. Americans should be offended that statistics are being used to diminish the crimes committed against their fellow citizens by narco-terrorists.

Let me be clear, this is happening on our side of the border and each day that they threaten a farmer or rancher, they get closer to impacting our nation's food supply.

American agriculture produces the safest, most affordable and most reliable food and fiber supply in the world – and Texas is a major contributor to those production efforts. Despite an ongoing drought and raging wildfires, the Texas agriculture industry has shown significant strengths in a trying time for the U.S. economy. We continue to lead the nation in the production of cattle, cotton, sheep, goats, mohair and many other products that American consumers rely on daily. Agriculture is also a significant sector of the Texas economy, producing an economic impact of about $100 billion a year. Mexico is the No. 2 export market for the United States and our No. 3 source of imports. It is this legal trade that we seek to preserve.

Let me give you a snapshot of the grave danger Texans face due to an insecure border. These are only some of the acts of violence these transnational criminal organizations have taken in the past few months:

- On Feb. 18 – Two energy company employees were assaulted and robbed in rural Webb County
- On March 11 – A ranch foreman was injured from shots fired by suspected drug cartel members in rural Webb County
- On June 9 – Texas DPS and Game Wardens were shot at by drug traffickers in rural Hidalgo County
- On June 19 – U.S. Border Patrol was shot at by drug traffickers in an area that has seen repeated shootings aimed at U.S. law enforcement in Hidalgo County

- On July 14 – Shots fired at water district workers in rural Hidalgo County
- On Sept. 27 – Shots fired, killing at least one individual, on Hidalgo County highway
- The personal testimony of the farmers, ranchers and employees being told to "turn around, look the other way, leave your property, or else," while cartel members run drugs and humans through private Texas properties.

All of these incidents – which law enforcement believes were caused by criminals linked to the cartels – have taken place this year, not on the southern side of the border as many would have you believe, but rather on American soil in Texas. We cannot allow the livelihoods and peaceful enjoyment of private property to continue to be jeopardized. We cannot allow our standards to devolve to a new tolerance threshold for violence against private property owners. In addition to acts of violence, Texans are witnessing the direct consequences of narco-terrorism and organized crime. Rural residents experience the human tragedy of finding dead bodies on their properties – those of the sick and frail who fell behind and were left to die by the traffickers. These well-documented cases are proof that these terrorists do not shed their label simply by stepping into the United States to bring organized crime and traffic drugs, people, weapons, and money.

We've heard of farmers selling out and closing their operations. We are talking about our domestic food supply. We cannot stand by and watch terrorists frighten farmers out of agriculture. We do not like being dependent on foreign oil; we must not become dependent on foreign food.

Transnational terrorists do not send their activity reports to the Homeland Security Secretary. We all know drug trafficking and human smuggling is occurring at alarming rates. During the Super Bowl in Dallas this past year, the Texas Attorney General's office focused resources to assist local law enforcement in combating underage prostitution and concerned faith-based organizations led a campaign during the Super Bowl to bring awareness to this issue. Are we really pretending there is not a problem?

We all know the transnational criminal activity has been heading to our border. What I'm telling you today is they are here, they have arrived and we need to stop making excuses, stop blaming each other and stop this incursion before the violence statistics exceed the naysayer's thresholds of tolerance. I for one have no tolerance for these transnational criminals trespassing on the soil, the sovereignty and the rights of the United States of America

The reality is our porous border is a problem for all Americans – not just those at the border. Law enforcement in New York, Los Angeles, Dallas and Houston have confirmed that cartels have gangs operating in these cities. How can the border be called secure when fierce assaults continue against American citizens on American soil; nightly incursions occur across Texas ranches; and dead bodies are scattered throughout private properties?

Unfortunately, the administration and others have repeatedly said the U.S.-Mexico border is "as secure now as it has ever been." While I acknowledge the progress and the gains made in urban border areas; the drugs in American cities and the cash flowing south say that interpretation is simply untrue. The increases in federal support have resulted in two scenarios along the Texas-Mexico border: 1) lower crime rates in urban border communities like Brownsville and El Paso, and 2) a rural runaround of the drug cartels now focusing their efforts where there is the weakest presence of federal border enforcement. Keep in mind that 93 percent of the land in counties along the Texas-Mexico border is unincorporated and overwhelmingly rural.

The bottom line is our border is not secure. What we have are transnational criminal organizations basing their operations in a foreign country and deploying military-type incursions on American soil. And our President indicates this is okay by saying we are more secure today? Members of Congress, please do not rest until we convince the President, an insecure border is an insecure America.

Texas is home to 64 percent of the U.S.-Mexico border, but only 44 percent of the Border Patrol agents. There are 14 Border Patrol agents per border mile on average from California to New Mexico. Yet there are less than half that many per mile in Texas at 6.2 agents per border mile. I assure you, and so do Generals McCaffrey and Scales in their report, there is no reason for Texas to have anything but a higher presence of federal law enforcement. One of which is to overturn and prevent a strategically beneficial, centrally located entry point for their drugs into the United States. The use of hub cities in Texas such as Austin and Dallas, already serve as gateways to transport drugs to markets across the U.S.

Each time the federal government denies there is a problem, only the cartels and traffickers benefit – they gain courage and territory. The federal government must act now and do more to protect America. Our lives and our livelihoods depend on a secure border where legal trade and commerce can grow. The entire border region is critical to the strength and future of Texas and our nation, and we need to see these communities prosper and economies grow without the threat of violence associated with illegal drug and human trafficking.

The federal government needs a smarter, dynamic response to avoid funneling this traffic into our rural areas. Texans want action and all Americans need action. The Texas Legislature, state and local law enforcement have invested considerable resources to support the mission of the U.S. Border Patrol and meet the public safety concerns of their constituents. These local, state and federal law enforcement officers are doing the best job they can, but ineffective federal policies have only allowed the problems to fester.

Our Border Patrol and local and state officers are doing the best job they can, but they are in dire need of the strategic support of our federal government to take the fight to the cartels and aid our neighbors to the south. The broader strategy our government is employing does not appear coordinated, effective or have the full attention of this administration to follow through in solving this problem.

To get that attention and respond to the urgent pleas for lifesaving help, I launched a website to document the real stories of Texans suffering from our insecure border. ProtectYourTexasBorder.com posts videos from those who have bravely come forward – in many cases anonymously for fear of retaliation – to share their encounters with these dangerous individuals. These are true accounts that document what is really happening on our side of the border. The evidence is clear; the border is not secure.

It is imperative the administration help us secure the border. On Monday, September 26th, I unveiled a detailed strategic assessment of the United States' southern border between Texas and Mexico that chronicles the impact of violent drug cartels and transnational criminal organizations. Co-authored by retired General Barry McCaffrey, the former Director of the Office of National Drug Control Policy under President Bill Clinton and the former Commander of all U.S. troops in Central and South America, and retired Major-General Robert Scales, the former Commandant of the United States Army War College, the assessment details the border problem in undeniable, stark terms. It also provides a strategic analysis of the danger and threat to our nation, and advocates for expanded resources and attention to secure the border.

Their assessment, along with many others that have genuinely looked at the war raging along our southern border, have concluded we cannot miss this opportunity to join with the Mexican government to confront narco-terrorism, by addressing the strategic needs this region requires to end the illegal flow of narcotics, people, guns and money.

Targeting these terrorists and securing the border only solves part of the problem; you also must address other weaknesses that have led to the abuse of our border and laws.

While I recognize these are two separate issues, it is undeniable that reducing the number of illegal entries into the U.S. by reforming our failed guest labor and immigration program would allow our law enforcement to focus resources on the remaining reduced illegal border crossings. Any expanded effort to secure the border would be benefited by substantially focusing on reforming a failed immigration system, which in turn would allow Border Patrol and law enforcement resources to be more fully engaged in stopping violent drug and human traffickers. All Americans, regardless of their background or culture, deserve a legal immigration system that meets our workforce needs and diminishes the demand for the coyote smugglers and traffickers who are exploiting and endangering lives.

Allowing a porous border is not only a threat to our citizens and nation's food supply, but also a threat to our homeland security. Clearly, such a threat stands in direct contrast to the protections authored by our Founding Fathers in the United States Constitution.

This debate can be summed up with one question: Would America allow terrorists based in Canada to make nightly incursions into New York? The answer is a resounding "No!" We need help and we need it now with the immediate deployment of additional boots on the ground.

Thank you for the opportunity to testify. I look forward to any questions you may have.

ENDNOTES

1   Webb County Sheriff Department. Patrol Division Supplementary Report filed March 7, 2011.
2   Personal testimony of a farm manager, corporate owners would not allow the name to be disclosed.
3   Dale Murden (Valley farmer and a state director of the Texas Farm Bureau). Personal Communication.
4   Ben Love. (West Texas rancher, and member, Texas and Southwestern Cattle Raisers Association). Personal Communication.
5   Condon, Stephanie. "Napolitano: Border security better than ever." *CBSNews.com*, 10:42 AM, March 25, 2011.
6   The Associated Press. "Obama mocks GOP, jokes they want border moat." *CBSNews.com*, 3:47PM, May 10, 2011.
7   Merriam-Webster, An Encyclopaedia Britannica Company. www.m-w.com. 2012.
8   ushistory.org, The Independence Hall Assocation (Philadelphia, PA), "The Electric Franklin." www.ushistory.org/franklin/info/index.htm.
9   Ibid.
10 Taylor, Jr., Dr. Quintard. University of Washington, Department of History. http://faculty.washington.edu/qtaylor/a_us_history/1700_1800_timeline.htm.

[11] Alan Axelrod, *1001 Events That Made America: A Patriot's Handbook*, (Washington, DC: National Geographic Society, 2006), 40.

[12] National FFA Organization, "www.ffa.org."

[13] National FFA Organization, Email Correspondence.

[14] U.S. National Park Service, "www.nps.gov."

[15] William W. Beach, and Patrick D. Tyrrell, "The 2012 Index of Dependence on Government," A Report of the Heritage Center for Data Analysis, The Heritage Foundation Leadership for America, SR-104. February 8, 2012, 2.

[16] United States Census Bureau, "census.gov." http://www.census.gov/foreign-trade/statistics/highlights/top/top1112yr.html.

[17] Ibid.

[18] Alejandro Figueroa, Erik Lee, Rick Van Schoik, "Realizing the Full Value of Crossborder Trade with Mexico," (Tempe, AZ: North American Center for Transborder Studies, 2011), 8.

[19] Ibid.

[20] Ibid., 9.

[21] Ibid., 3.

[22] Cave, Damien. "Crossing Over, and Over. Migrant shelters along the Mexican border are filled with seasoned crossers: older men and women, often deportees, braving ever-greater risks to get back to their families in the United States–the country they consider their home." *NYTimes.com*, October 2, 2011.

[23] At the time Walker attended, it was known as The Agricultural & Mechanical College of Texas.

24 www.aggietraditions.tamu.edu and W.D. "Bill" Walker Jr., (WWII Veteran and former student of Texas A&M University). Personal Communication.

25 John A. Garraty, *The American Nation: A History of the United States*. Second Edition, (New York: American Heritage Publishing Co., 1971).

26 Peter Jennings, and Todd Brewster, *The Century*, (New York: Bantam Doubleday Dell Publishing Group, Inc., 1998), 239-240.

27 John A. Garraty, *The American Nation: A History of the United States*. Second Edition, (New York: American Heritage Publishing Co., 1971), 877.

28 Walter E. Williams, *Race and Economics: How Much Can Be Blamed on Discrimination?*, (Stanford: Hoover Institution Press, 2011), 3.

29 Ibid, 52.

30 Adam Smith qtd. in Ibid, 59.

31 Ibid., 62-63.

32 Alan Axelrod, *1001 Events That Made America: A Patriot's Handbook*, (Washington, DC: National Geographic Society, 2006), 57.

33 Dumas Malone, and Basil Rauch, *The Republic Comes of Age 1789-1841*, (New York: Appleton-Century-Crofts, 1960), 71.

34 Seib, Gerald F. "In Crisis, Opportunity for Obama." *Wall Street Journal, online.wsj.com*, US edition. November 21, 2008.

35 Dumas Malone, and Basil Rauch, *The Republic Comes of Age 1789-1841*, (New York: Appleton-Century-Crofts, 1960), 71.

36 Ibid.

37 Rebecca Brooks Gruver, *An American History*. Third Edition, (New York: Addison-Wesley Publishing Company, 1981), 176-177.

38 Schwartz, John. "Supreme Court Decision on Arizona Immigration Law." *New York Times, NYTimes.com*, June 26, 2012.

39 Preston, Julia. "Arizona Ruling Only a Narrow Opening for Other States." *New York Times, NYTimes.com*, June 25, 2012.

40 Wallsten, Peter. "U.S. will stop deporting some illegal immigrants who came here as children." *The Washington Post*. June 15, 2012.

41 Bureau of Labor Statistics, U.S. Department of Labor, The Editor's Desk, Unemployment in June 2012. http://www.bls.gov/opub/ted/2012/ted_20120710.htm .

42 Texas Association of Business, "txbiz.org." http://www.txbiz.org/advocacy/immigration.aspx.

43 Georgia Department of Agriculture. "Report on Agriculture Labor." January 2012.

44 Freeman, James. "The Bullish Case for the U.S. Economy." *Wall Street Journal, online.wsj.com*, June 4, 2011.

45 Ibid.

46 Board of Governors of the Federal Reserve. "Consumers and Mobile Financial Services," www.federalreserve.gov. March 2012.

47 USDA-Economic Research Service, "Food Expenditures." Last modified December 14, 2012. http://www.ers.usda.gov/data-products/food-expenditures.aspx. Table97_2011.

[48] USDA-Economic Research Service, "Food Expenditures." Last modified December 14, 2012. http://www.ers.usda.gov/data-products/food-expenditures.aspx. Table 7.

[49] USDA-Economic Research Service, 2010 import and export data, http://www.ers.usda.gov/topics/international-markets-trade/us-agricultural-trade/import-share-of-consumption.aspx.

[50] Eric Foner, and John A. Garraty, *The Reader's Companion to American History*, (Boston: Houghton Mifflin, 1991), 536-537.

[51] "U.S. Immigration Since 1965," The History Channel website, http://www.history.com/topics/us-immigration-since-1965.

[52] Ibid.

[53] Walter E. Williams, *Race and Economics: How Much Can Be Blamed on Discrimination?*, (Stanford: Hoover Institution Press, 2011), 3.

[54] Balz, Dan. "Who Shot Mike Martin?", *Spokesman-Review,* Spokane, Washington. August 30, 1981. Reprint.

[55] Aguilar, Julian. "On State Website, Calls for Vigilante Justice." *Texas Tribune, texastribune. org*, March 9, 2011. http://www.texastribune.org/texas-mexico-border-news/texas-mexico-border/on-state-website-calls-for-vigilante-justice/

[56] Payne, Douglas W. "The Drug Lords of Maverick County." *New York Times*, July 27, 1997.

[57] James Francis, (former Chairman of the Texas Public Safety Commission), Personal Communication.

58 *DPS Chaparral,* DPS Public Information, August 2009.

59 "DPS commends local and federal law enforcement agencies in Texas for seizing over $8 billion in drugs and cash." Public Affairs Office, Texas Department of Public Safety, October 12, 2011.

60 Texas Department of Public Safety, www.txdps. state.tx.us.   http://www.txdps.state.tx.us/Public Information/operDrawbrdg.htm

61 "Commissioner Staples applauds DPS for protecting landowners by leveraging technology to fight drug, human trafficking." *PR News Channel, prnewschannel.com,* June 21, 2012. http://www. prnewschannel.com/2012/06/21/commissioner-staples-applauds-dps-for-protecting-landowners-by-leveraging-technology-to-fight-drug-human-trafficking/.

62 "Mexican Cartel Related Activity." Texas Department of Public Safety, www.txdps.state.tx.us. http://www.txdps.state.tx.us/PublicInformation/cartelCrimeStats.htm

63 Farley, Robert. "Obama says border patrol has doubled the number of agents since 2004." *Tampa Bay Times,* May 10, 2011.

64 Yockelson, Mitchell. "The United States Armed Forces and the Mexican Punitive Expedition, Part 1." *Prologue Magazine, Fall 1997, Vol. 29, No. 3.*

65 Barry R. McCaffrey, and Robert H. Scales PhD, "Texas Border Security: A Strategic Military Assessment," (Austin, TX: Texas Department of Agriculture, 2011).

66 "Border Patrol Troops Snap Shot." www. ProtectYourTexasBorder.com. http://protectyour texasborder.com/Portals/6/Infographic%202%20 Final.jpg

67 Novick, Daniel. "Website Created By Texas Agriculture Commissioner Raises Awareness About Border Security." *CW33 News*, March 15, 2012.

68 Ibid.

69 Barry R. McCaffrey, and Robert H. Scales PhD, "Texas Border Security: A Strategic Military Assessment," (Austin, TX: Texas Department of Agriculture, 2011).

70 U.S. Census Bureau, USA Trade Online Database. www.usatradeonline.gov.

71 Sherman, Christopher. "Border violence spills onto Mexican ranches." Associated Press. *Lubbock Avalanche-Journal, lubbockonline.com*, July 8, 2010.

72 Ibid.

73 GAO, Border Security: Preliminary Observations on Border Control Measures for the Southwest Border, GAO-11-374T, (Washington, DC: Feb 15, 2011).

74 Ibid.

75 Ibid.

76 Ibid.

77 FBI, "UCR General FAQs." http://www.fbi.gov/ about-us/cjis/ucr/frequently-asked-questions/ ucr_faqs.

78 FBI, "Caution against ranking: Variables Affecting Crime." http://www2.fbi.gov/ucr/cius2009/about/ variables_affecting_crime.html.

79 Beittel, June S., *Mexico's Drug Trafficking Organizations: Source and Scope of the Rising Violence.* Congressional Research Service, August 3, 2012.

80 Potter, Mark. "Debate rages over Mexico 'spillover violence' in U.S." *NBC Nightly News*, March 15, 2012.

81 "Mexican Cartel Related Activity." DPS Newsroom, www.txdps.state.tx.us. http://www.txdps.state.tx.us/PublicInformation/cartelCrimeStats.htm

82 Ibid.

83 House Immigration Reform Caucus. "A Field Investigation Report of the House Immigration Reform Caucus." November 19, 2010.

84 Potter, Mark. "Debate rages over Mexico 'spillover violence' in U.S." *NBC Nightly News*, March 15, 2012.

85 Alexis de Tocqueville, *Democracy In America.* Translated by George Lawrence. (New York: Harper Perennial Modern Classics, 1998)

86 Ibid., 36.

87 Ibid.

88 Ibid., 32-40.

89 Rebecca Brooks Gruver, *An American History.* Third Edition, (New York: Addison-Wesley Publishing Company, 1981), 490-493.

90 Ibid., 490-493.

91 Houston Chronicle, chron.com. blog.chron.com/texas/politics/2011/09/border-congressman-blasts-report-on-border-violence/ and http://reyes.house.gov/news/documentprint.aspx?DocumentID=262053.

[92] Meese, Edwin III. "An Amnesty By Any Other Name." The New York Times, May 24, 2006

[93] Bennett, George. "Rubio: Regan erred in supporting 1986 amnesty for illegal immigrants." Post on Politics. *The Palm Beach Post*. November 17, 2009.

[94] H.R. 2124, 112th Congress, Francisco "Quinco" Canseco.

[95] Department of Homeland Security, www.dhs.gov.

[96] Judicial Watch "Judicial Watch Obtains New Border Patrol Apprehension Statistics for Illegal Alien Smugglers and 'Special Interest Aliens'." www. judicialwatch.com. http://www.prnewswire.com/ news-releases/judicial-watch-obtains-new-border-patrol-apprehension-statistics-for-illegal-alien-smugglers-and-special-interest-aliens-117673378. html.

[97] Ibid.

[98] 2010 Census, 2010. Census.gov/2010census/data/ apportionment-pop-text.php.

[99] U.S. Department of State. Employment-Based Immigrant Visas and Types of Visas for Temporary Visitors. http://travel.state.gov/visa/temp/types/ types_1286.html.

[100] New H2B Rules Provide Better Security for Workers and Employers, Immigrationdirect.com. February 23, 2012.

[101] Ibid.

[102] Rust, Sean "Why Market Based Immigration is America's Best Bet." Forbes, June 27, 2012.

[103] U.S. Census Bureau, U.S. and World Population Clock. www.census.gov/main/www/popclock.html.

[104] Cave, Damien. "Changing face of migration on display at border," *The Seattle Times*. Reprint. October 8, 2011. (Original print: "Crossing Over, and Over. Migrant shelters along the Mexican border are filled with seasoned crossers: older men and women, often deportees, braving ever-greater risks to get back to their families in the United States–the country they consider their home." NYTimes.com, October 2, 2011.)

[105] Alejandro Figueroa, Erik Lee, Rick Van Schoik, Realizing the Full Value of Crossborder Trade with Mexico, (Tempe, AZ: North American Center for Transborder Studies, 2011), 11.

[106] Ibid.

[107] Transcript provided by the website of Michelle Malkin. http://michellemalkin.com/2008/06/27/lonesome-dove-explained/.

[108] Sylvia Longmire, *Cartel*. (New York: Palgrave MacMillan, 2011). 10.

[109] Associated Press, Michael Weissenstein, Friday, July 6, 2012.

[110] Ibid.

[111] "Mexican Cartel Related Activity." Texas Department of Public Safety, www.txdps.state.tx.us. http://www.txdps.state.tx.us/PublicInformation/cartelCrimeStats.htm.

[112] The Price of Mexico's "drug war" by Julian Miglierini, BBC News, April 18, 2011.

[113] Ibid.

[114] Sarukhan, Arturo. Letters to the Editor, *Dallas Morning News*, April 11, 2011.

[115] Staples, Todd. Letters to the Editor, *Dallas Morning News*, April 14, 2011.

[116] Congressional Hearing testimony. www.ProtectYourTexasBorder.com. October 14, 2011.

[117] "Don't Raise the Debt Limit Without Getting Spending Under Control," Heritage Foundation, Heritage.org, April 21, 2011.